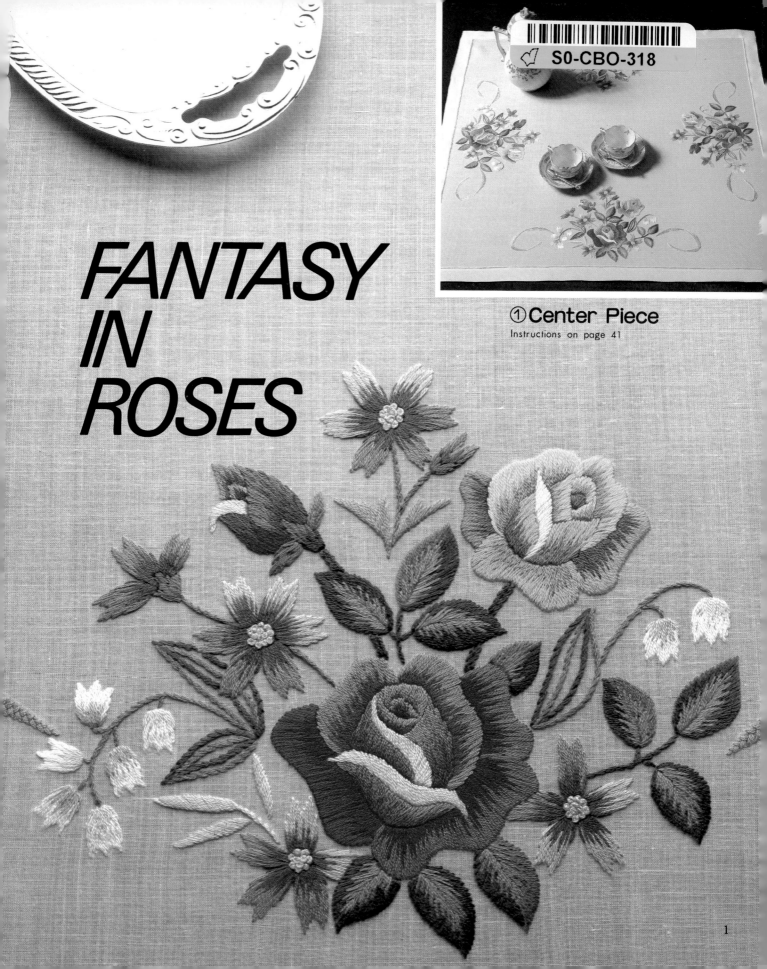

FANTASY IN ROSES

① **Center Piece**

Instructions on page 41

1

②Tablecloth & Napkin

Instructions on page 46

2

③Center Piece
Instructions on page 44

4

④Pillow
Instructions on page 55

⑤ **Tablecloth**
Instructions on page 43

⑥,⑦ **Pillows**
Instructions on page 48

⑥

⑦

8

⑧ Piano Throw
Instructions on page 50

10

IMPRESSION OF WHITE

12

⑪ Center Piece

Instructions on page 57

⑫ **Center Piece**
Instructions on page 54

⑬,⑭,⑮,⑯ Handkerchieves

Instructions on pages 57, 60, 61, 60

⑭

⑬

⑮

⑯

⑰ Dolly
Instructions on page 64

18

⑱ **Tablecloth**
Instructions on page 66

⑲ **Curtain**
Instructions on page 68

CROSS STITCH IN LIVING

⑳Pillows
Instructions on page 72

㉑**Pillows**
Instructions on page 73

㉒**Pillows**
Instructions on page 83

㉓Center Piece
Instructions on page 74

㉔ Framed Picture

Instructions on page 70

A WALTZ OF FLOWERS

26 **Center Piece**
Instructions on page 79

28

㉗**Tablecloth**

Instructions on page 78

㉛ Center Piece
Instructions on page 86

34

㉜ Doily
Instructions on page 88

㉝ Doily
Instructions on page 92

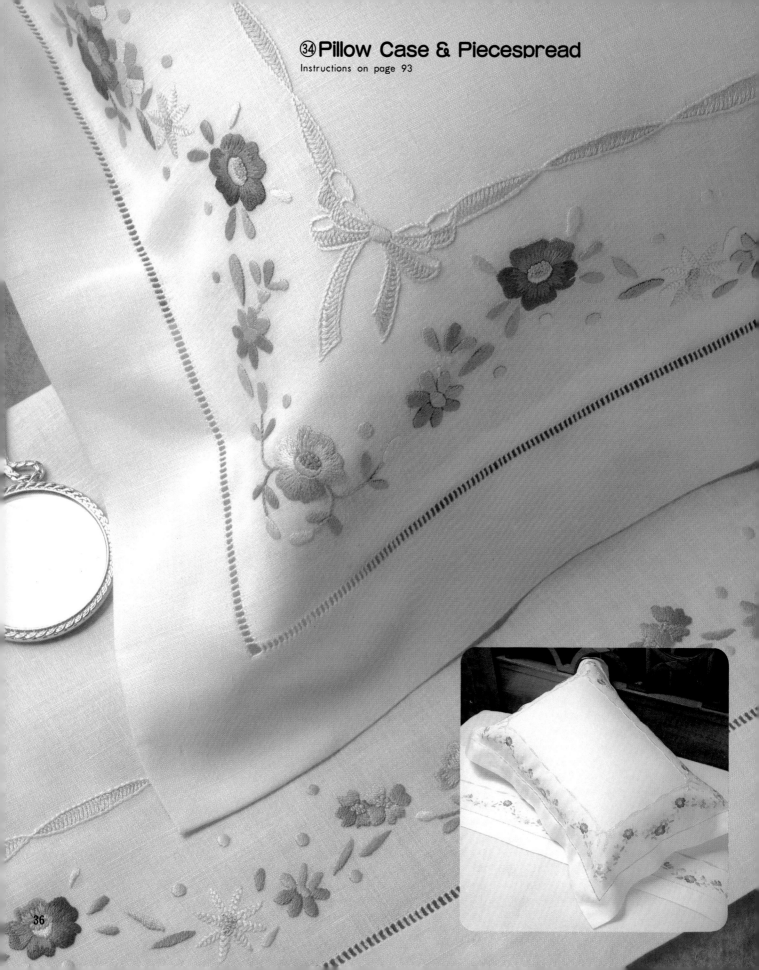

㉞ **Pillow Case & Piecespread**
Instructions on page 93

㉟ **Pillow**
Instructions on page 97

FLOWERING PLANTS

㉟, ㉙ Mini Pictures
Instructions on page 100

㊳,㊴ Mini Pictures
Instructions on page 100

㊵,㊶ Mini Pictures
Instructions on page 100

MAKING INSTRUCTIONS

---

①CENTER PIECE shown on page 1

You'll Need:

- Fabric . . . White linen 85 cm square.
- Threads . . . D.M.C 6-strand embroidery floss:
  2 skeins each of Garnet Red (309), Magenta Rose (961);
  1½ skeins each of Garnet Red (326), Parma Violet (209, 211); 1 skein each of Soft Pink (899), Violet Mauve (327), Ash Grey (762), Yellow Green (730), White; ½ skein each of Magenta Rose (963), Golden Yellow (780, 782, 783), Saffron (725, 726), Light Yellow (3078), Indian Red (3042), Umber (739), Ash Grey (415), Moss Green (937, 471), Sage Green (3012, 3013), Ivy Green (501) and Almond Green (502).

Finished Size: 75 cm square

Making Instructions:

Transfer design on each side in the middle, stitch embroidery. Work outline st along the edge, fold cut edge twice, finish mitering at corners.

Chart of measurement

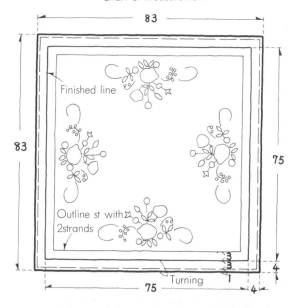

Flower

● = 326
◄ = 309
⊠ = 961
∨ = 899
■ = 780
□ = 782
○ = 783
△ = 725
✕ = 726
‡ = 209
T = 211
◉ = 415
∅ = 762

Leaf, stalk, calyx

A = 937
B = 730
C = 3012
D = 3013
E = 471

Satin

Satin (3078)

French knot filling
(739)

(327)

(3042)

B

Outline

B

Outline — B

Outline
B

Satin D

Outline
B

Outline
B

Outline — B

A E D

Satin (963)

Satin (963)

Center

Closed herringbone

(Actual size)

Long and short st unless specified. 2
strands for the inward of long and short
st of flowers & leaves, 3 strands for the
rest.

Satin
(963)

(3042)

Outline

C

Outline
C

Satin   Outline
{
(739)

(White)

Outline { (501)
          (502)

(White) } Outline
(762)

Ⓐ

Ⓐ

42

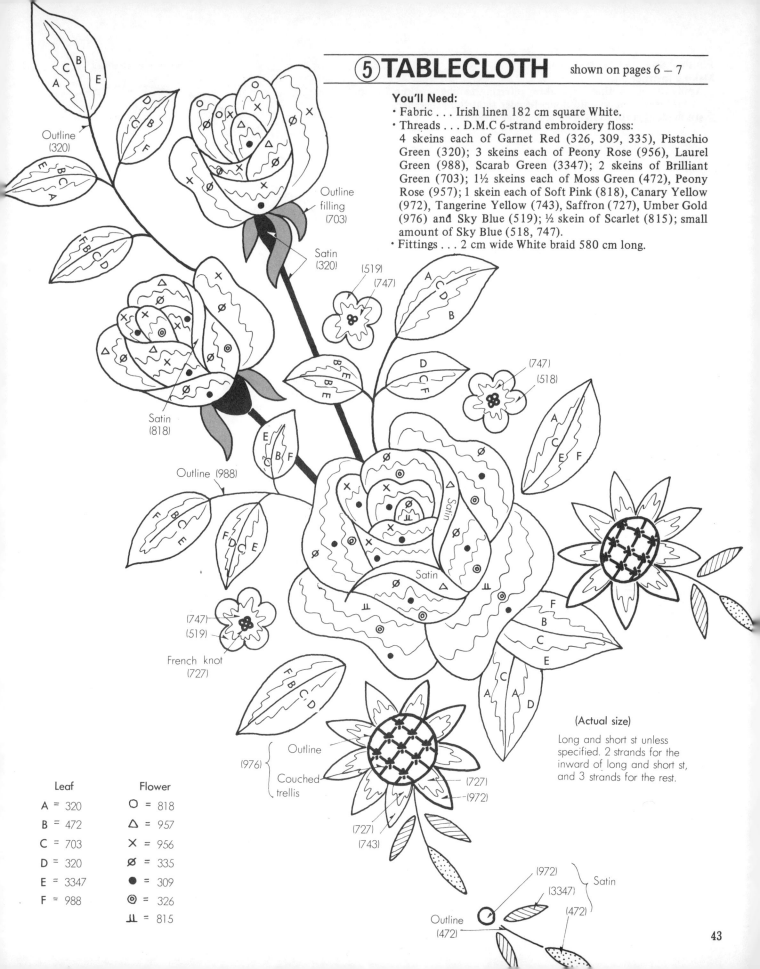

You'll Need:
· Fabric . . . Irish linen 182 cm square White.
· Threads . . . D.M.C 6-strand embroidery floss:
  4 skeins each of Garnet Red (326, 309, 335), Pistachio Green (320); 3 skeins each of Peony Rose (956), Laurel Green (988), Scarab Green (3347); 2 skeins of Brilliant Green (703); 1½ skeins each of Moss Green (472), Peony Rose (957); 1 skein each of Soft Pink (818), Canary Yellow (972), Tangerine Yellow (743), Saffron (727), Umber Gold (976) and Sky Blue (519); ½ skein of Scarlet (815); small amount of Sky Blue (518, 747).
· Fittings . . . 2 cm wide White braid 580 cm long.

Outline
(320)

Outline
filling
(703)

Satin
(320)

(519)
(747)

(747)
(518)

Satin
(818)

Outline (988)

Satin

Satin

(747)
(519)

French knot
(727)

(976)

Outline

Couched
trellis

(727)
(972)

(727)
(743)

(Actual size)

Long and short st unless specified. 2 strands for the inward of long and short st, and 3 strands for the rest.

(972)

(3347)   Satin

(472)

Outline
(472)

Leaf		Flower	
A =	320	O =	818
B =	472	△ =	957
C =	703	✕ =	956
D =	320	∅ =	335
E =	3347	● =	309
F =	988	◎ =	326
		⊥⊥ =	815

Finished Size: 181 cm in diameter

Making Instructions:

Apply design 8 times on fabric referring to chart, stitch embroidery. Apply braid along the edge right sides together, stitch along, turn to right side, machine steady.

Finishing with Braid

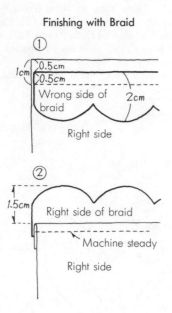

Chart of measurement

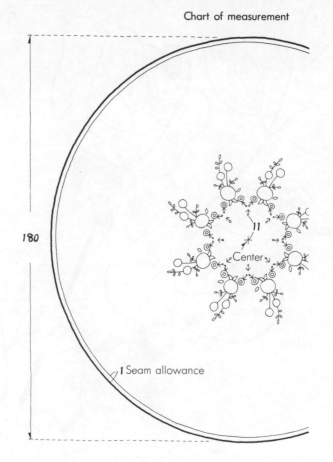

③CENTER PIECE shown on page 4

You'll Need:

- Fabric ... Irish linen 66 cm by 43 cm Off-White.
- Threads ... D.M.C 6-strand embroidery floss:
  1 skein each of Canary Yellow (971), Tangerine Yellow (740, 741), Fire Red (900, 946, 947), Turkey Red (321), Forget-me-not Blue (826), Azure Blue (3325), Sage Green (3012, 3013), Moss Green (936, 937); ½ skein each of Geranium Red (754), Forget-me-not Blue (925, 827) and Golden Yellow (783); small amount of Geranium Red (754).

Finished Size: 60 cm by 37 cm

Making Instructions:

Referring to chart, transfer design on fabric symmetrically, stitch embroidery.

Turn out edge twice, steady with both-side hem-stitching, mitering at each corner.

Chart of measurement

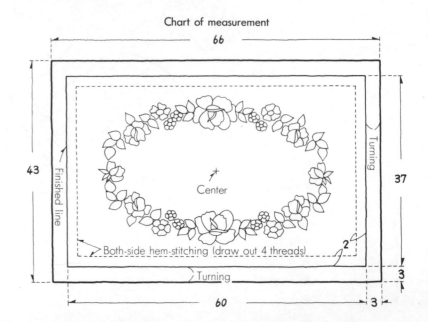

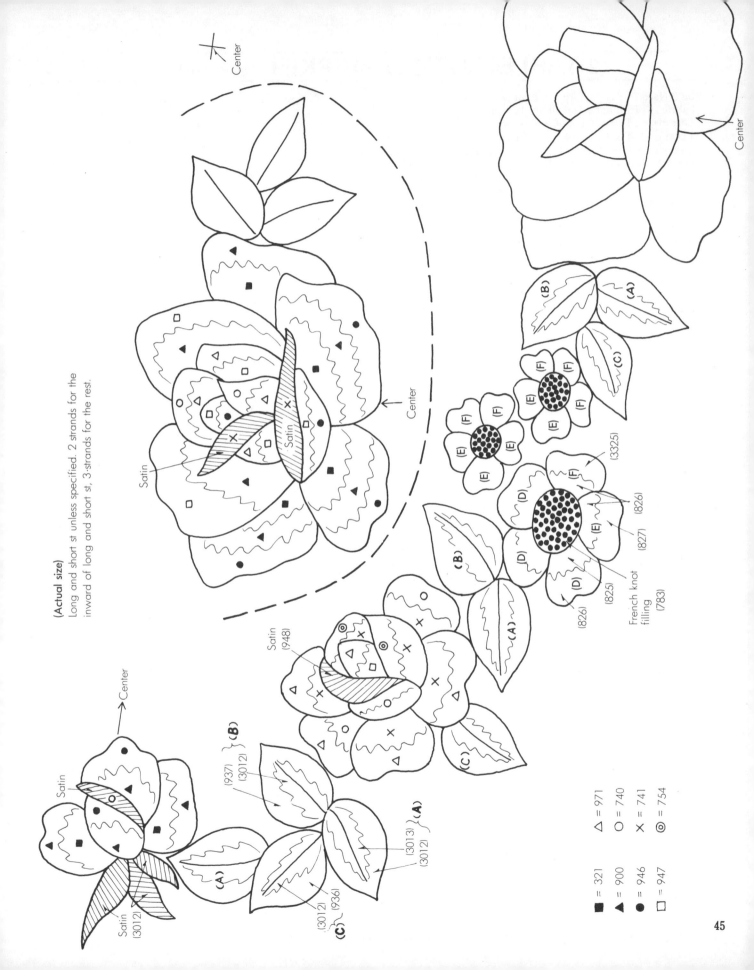

(Actual size)
Long and short st unless specified. 2 strands for the inward of long and short st, 3-strands for the rest.

Center

Satin

Satin

Satin

Center

Center

Center

(B)

(A)

(C)

(E) (F) (F)

(E) (F)

(E) (E)

(E) (F)

(E)

(3325)

(F)

(D)

(D)

(E)

(826)

(827)

(826)

French knot filling
(783)

(D)

(825)

(826)

(B)

(A)

Satin
(948)

(B)

(937)
(3012)

(A)

(3013)
(3012)

(3012)

(C)

(C)

(3012)
(936)

Satin
(3012)

Satin

Center

(A)

■ = 321
▲ = 900
● = 946
□ = 947

△ = 971
○ = 740
✕ = 741
◎ = 754

45

②TABLECLOTH & NAPKIN

shown on pages 2 — 3

You'll Need (for tablecloth and 2 pieces of napkin):
· Fabric . . . Irish linen 166 cm by 160 cm Ivory.
· Threads . . . D.M.C 6-strand embroidery floss:
  4 skeins of Moss Green (471); 3 skeins of Moss Green (470);
  2 skeins each of Saffron (725, 727), Canary Yellow (972),
  Light Yellow (3078); 1½ skeins each of Tangerine Yellow
  (743), Laurel Green (988); 1 skein each of Golden Yellow
  (780, 783), Saffron (726), Cream (746), Tangerine Yellow
  (740, 741), Red Brown (921), Yellow Green (733), Moss
  Green (469) and Scarab Green (3348).
· Fittings . . . 2 cm wide Yellow braid 950 cm long.
Finished Size: Tablecloth 161 cm by 122 cm
  Napkin 46 cm square
Making Instructions:
Copy design referring to chart, stitch embroidery.
Apply braid along the edge of fabric right sides together,
machine 0.5 cm off the edge, turn to right side, machine
steady.

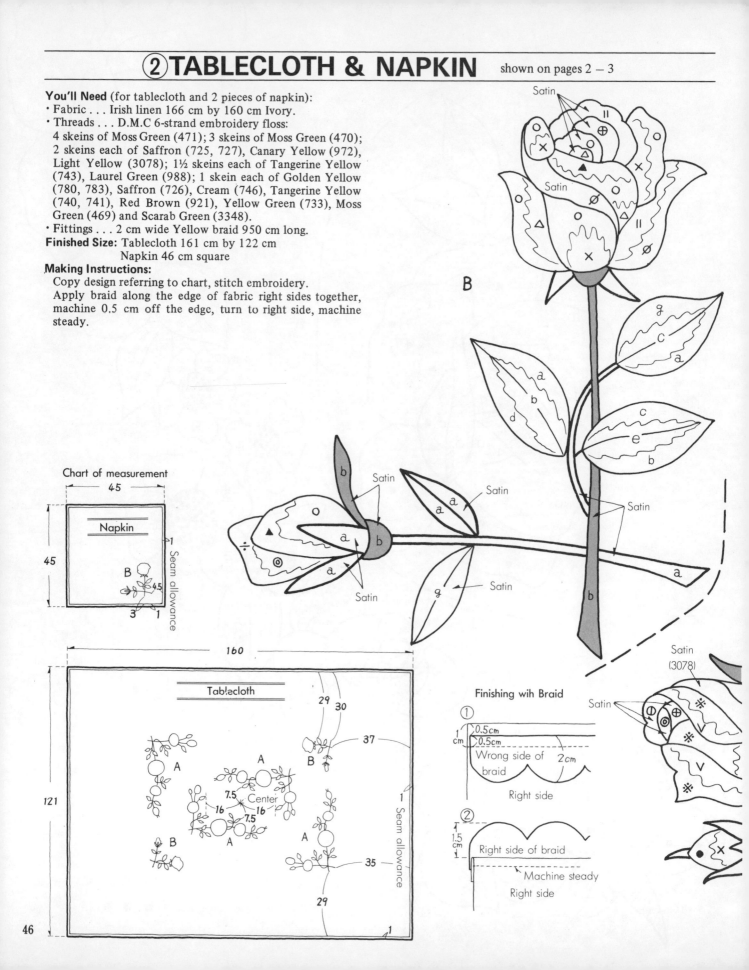

(Actual size)
Long and short st unless specified.
With 3 strands.

a = 471
b = 470
c = 988
d = 733
e = 469
g = 3348
※ = 725
o = 972
‖ = 743
◎ = 780
÷ = 783
Ⓘ = 726
V = 727
▲ = 727
Ø = 3078
⊕ = 746
● = 741
× = 740
△ = 921

A

Satin

Outline
a

Satin

Satin

Outline
b

Satin

(3078)

Satin

Satin

Satin

Satin

Satin

Satin

47

⑥⑦PILLOWS shown on pages 8 — 9

You'll Need (for 2 portions):
- Fabrics . . . Irish linen 36 cm by 37 cm Off-White. Wool georgette 142 cm by 78 cm Moss Green.
- Threads . . . D.M.C 6-strand embroidery floss:
  ⑥ 1 skein each of Golden Yellow (783), Saffron (725, 726, 727), Yellow Green (730); small amount each of Golden Yellow (782), Light Yellow (3078), Moss Green (937), Laurel Green (986, 988), Parrakeet Green (904), Scarab Green (3347, 3348) and Brilliant Green (701, 702)
  ⑦ 1 skein each of Scarlet (304), Geranium Red (817, 350, 351), Yellow Green (730); small amount each of Cardinal Red (347), Morocco Red (761), Moss Green (936, 937, 469, 470, 471, 472) and Brilliant Green (701, 702)

- Fittings . . . 2 of 28 cm long zip fastener. 2 of 37 cm square inner case stuffed with 300 g. kapok.

Finished Size: Refer to chart.

Making Instructions:
Cut Irish linen in size (18 cm by 37 cm), copy design, stitch embroidery. Work smocking on side strips in front. Bind side edges of the center piece front, join to side pieces. Set zip fastener in place on back, put front and back right sides together, finish edges with bias binding.

Chart of measurement
Georgette unless specified.

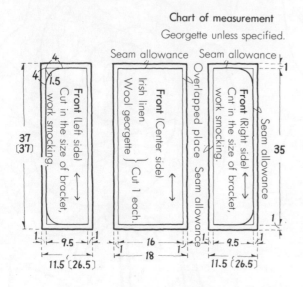

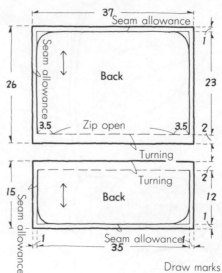

Cutting Georgette (for 2 portions):

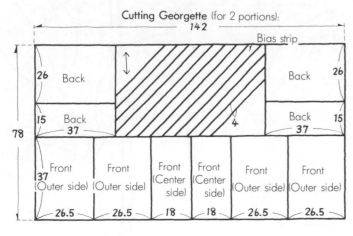

Smocking on Left & Right in Front
Draw marks on wrong side of fabric, smock wrong side with 4 strands.

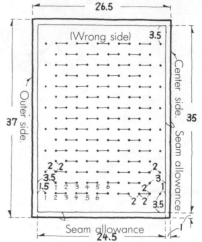

Smocking

② Insert needle at the interval of 0.2cm to 1, bring needle to 2.

③ Stitch 3 to 4. Be sure not to draw the thread between 2 and 3 tightly.

④ Bring needle to 3 at the interval of 0.2 cm, back to 4 at the interval of 0.2 cm, keeping the previous stitch steady.

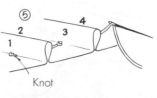

Knot

⑤ Repeat ③-⑤.

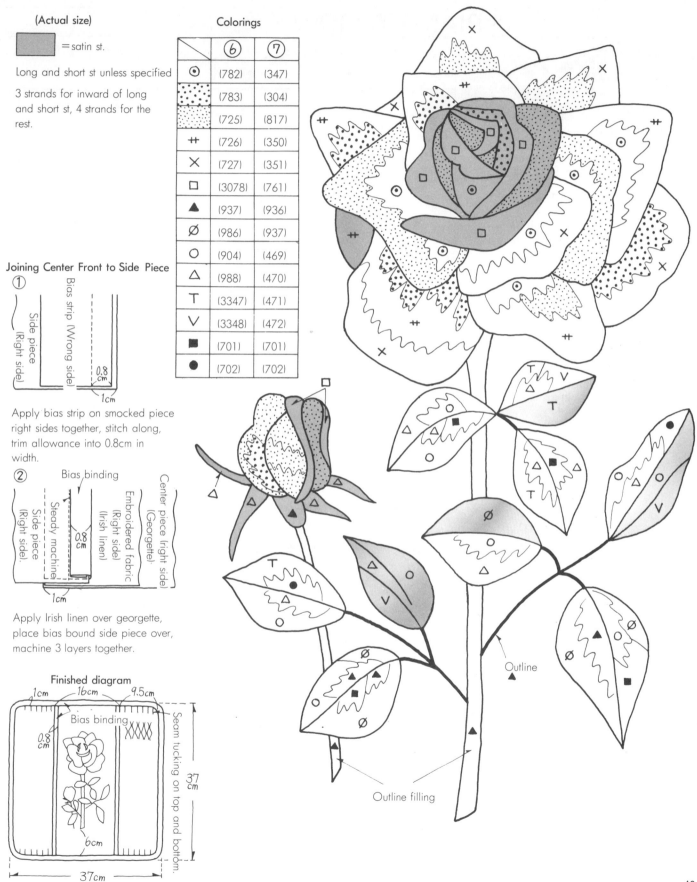

(Actual size)

◼ = satin st.

Long and short st unless specified

3 strands for inward of long and short st, 4 strands for the rest.

Colorings

	⑥	⑦
⊙	(782)	(347)
⠿	(783)	(304)
⠄	(725)	(817)
╫	(726)	(350)
×	(727)	(351)
□	(3078)	(761)
▲	(937)	(936)
Ø	(986)	(937)
O	(904)	(469)
△	(988)	(470)
T	(3347)	(471)
V	(3348)	(472)
■	(701)	(701)
●	(702)	(702)

Joining Center Front to Side Piece

① Side piece (Right side) Bias strip (Wrong side) 0.8 cm 1cm

Apply bias strip on smocked piece right sides together, stitch along, trim allowance into 0.8cm in width.

② Bias binding Side piece (Right side) Steady machine Embroidered fabric (Right side) (Irish linen) Center piece (right side) (Georgette) 0.8 cm 1cm

Apply Irish linen over georgette, place bias bound side piece over, machine 3 layers together.

Finished diagram

1cm 16cm 9.5cm Bias binding 0.8 cm Seam tucking on top and bottom. 37cm 6cm 37cm

Outline

Outline filling

You'll Need:
- Fabric . . . Irish linen 90 cm by 214 cm Off-White.
- Threads . . . D.M.C 6-strand embroidery floss:
3 skeins each of Light Yellow (3078), Moss Green (469), Laurel Green (988), Peony Rose (957); 2 skeins each of Garnet Red (335), Moss Green (937, 470, 472), Scarab Green (3347), Soft Pink (899); 1 skein each of Scarlet (902, 815), Garnet Red (326, 309), Cerise (602), Geranium Pink (894), Soft Pink (776, 818, 819), Golden Yellow (782, 783), Saffron (725, 727), Tangerine Yellow (743) and Moss Green (471).
- Fittings . . . 2 cm wide Off-White braid 400 cm long. White bias tape 240 cm long.

Finished Size: 211 cm by 87.5 cm

Making Instructions:
Transfer design referring to chart, stitch embroidery.
Finish both sides folding cut edge twice, bottom side using bias binding. Apply braid along the edge.

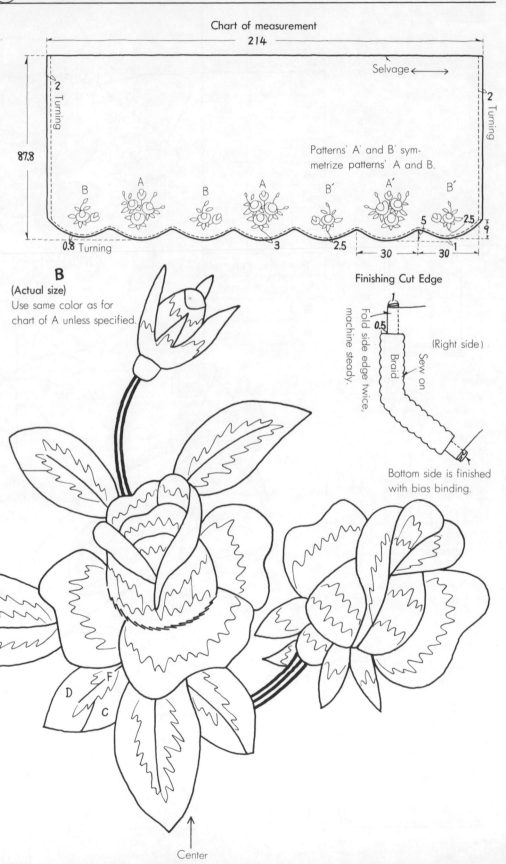

Chart of measurement

Selvage

Patterns' A' and B' symmetrize patterns' A and B.

B (Actual size)
Use same color as for chart of A unless specified.

Finishing Cut Edge

Fold side edge twice, machine steady.

(Right side)

Braid

Sew on

Bottom side is finished with bias binding.

Center

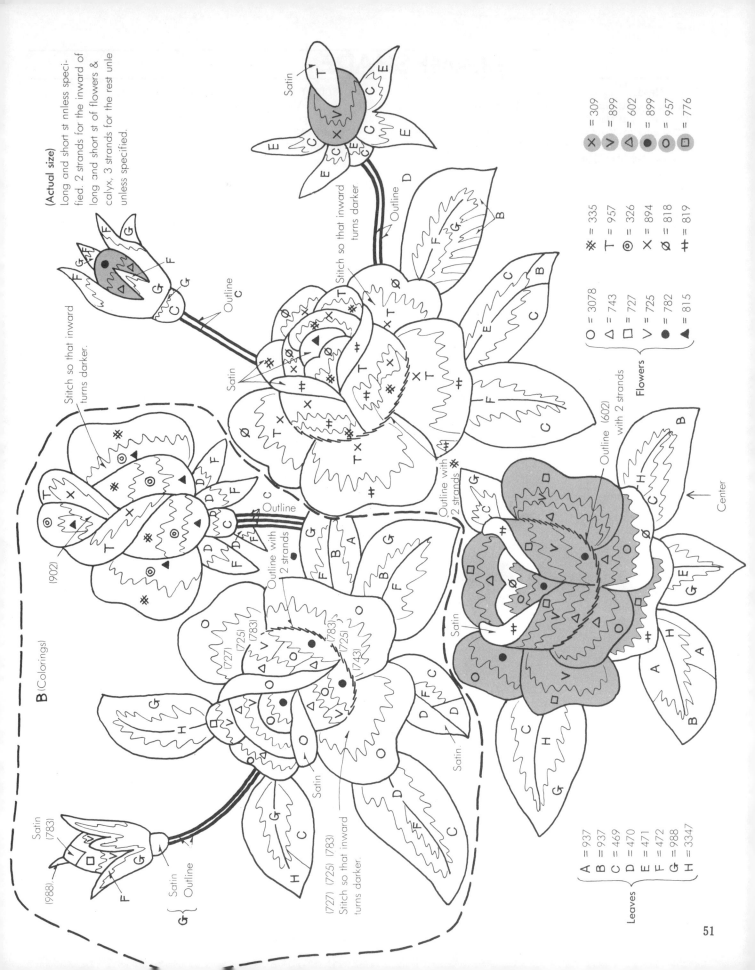

(Actual size)
Long and short st unless specified. 2 strands for the inward of long and short st of flowers & calyx, 3 strands for the rest unless specified.

Stitch so that inward turns darker.

Satin

Outline
C

Satin

Outline

Stitch so that inward turns darker.

Satin

Outline

Outline with 2 strands

Outline with 2 strands

Outline (602) with 2 strands

Center

Satin

B (Colorings)

(902)

(727) (725) (783)

(725) (783)
(725)
(727)
(783)
(743)

Satin
(783)

(988)

Satin
Outline

(727) (725) (783)
Stitch so that inward turns darker.

⊗	= 309
V	= 899
◁	= 602
●	= 899
○	= 957
▢	= 776

※	= 335
T	= 957
◎	= 326
✕	= 894
∅	= 818
✢	= 819

○	= 3078
△	= 743
▢	= 727
V	= 725
●	= 782
▲	= 815

Flowers

Leaves
A	= 937
B	= 937
C	= 469
D	= 470
E	= 471
F	= 472
G	= 988
H	= 3347

⑨LAMPSHADE   shown on page 11

You'll Need:
- Fabric . . . Irish linen 115 cm by 41 cm Off-White.
- Threads . . . D.M.C 6-strand embroidery floss:
  1½ skeins of Moss Green (470); 1 skein each of Soft Pink (899, 776, 819), Cerise (601), Laurel Green (988), Light Yellow (3078); ½ skein each of Moss Green (936, 469), Parrakeet Green (904), Scarab Green (3347, 3348), Pistachio Green (319), Saffron (727); small amount each of Garnet Red (335), Scarlet (814), Moss Green (472), Pistachio Green (367), Saffron (725, 726), Sevres Blue (799, 800), Forget-me-not Blue (828), Plum (552, 553, 554) and Parma Violet (211).
- Fittings . . . 2 cm wide White braid 225 cm long.

Finished Size: Refer to chart.

Making Instructions:
Transfer design referring to chart, stitch embroidery. Finish the work in shape at its specialty store.

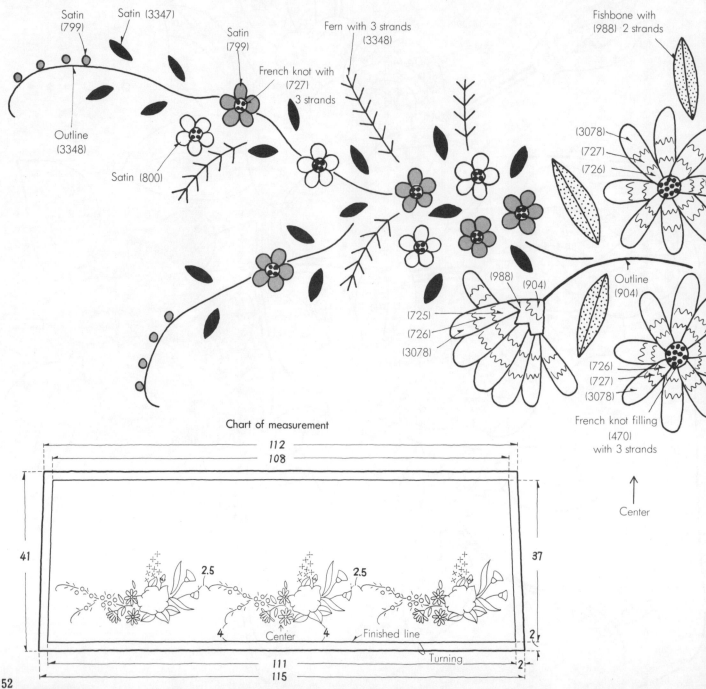

Chart of measurement

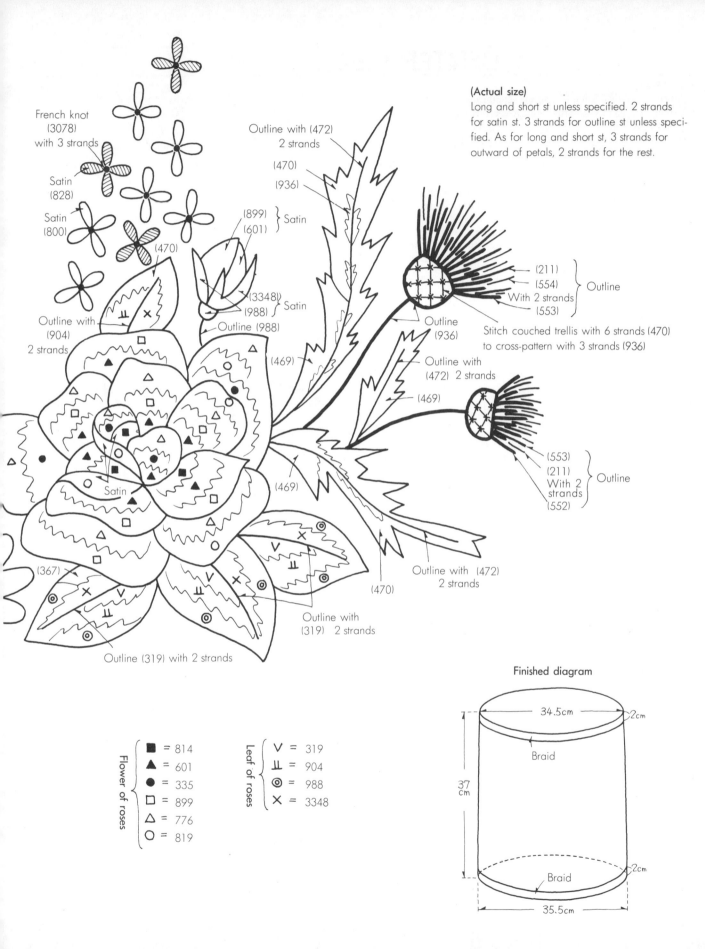

French knot
(3078)
with 3 strands

Satin
(828)

Satin
(800)

(470)

Outline with
(904)
2 strands

(367)

Outline (319) with 2 strands

Outline with (472)
2 strands

(470)

(936)

(899)
(601) } Satin

(3348)
(988) } Satin

Outline (988)

(899)
(601)

(469)

(469)

(469)

Outline with
(319) 2 strands

(Actual size)
Long and short st unless specified. 2 strands
for satin st. 3 strands for outline st unless specified. As for long and short st, 3 strands for
outward of petals, 2 strands for the rest.

Outline
(936)

(211)
(554)
With 2 strands
(553)

} Outline

Stitch couched trellis with 6 strands (470)
to cross-pattern with 3 strands (936)

Outline with
(472) 2 strands

(469)

(553)
(211)
With 2
strands
(552)

} Outline

Satin

Outline with (472)
2 strands

(470)

Flower of roses
■ = 814
▲ = 601
● = 335
□ = 899
△ = 776
○ = 819

Leaf of roses
V = 319
Ⱶ = 904
◎ = 988
X = 3348

Finished diagram

34.5cm
2cm

Braid

37 cm

Braid

2cm

35.5cm

53

⑫CENTER PIECE   shown on page 15

You'll Need:
- Fabric . . . White linen 75 cm by 45 cm.
- Threads . . . D.M.C 6-strnad embroidery floss:
  7 skeins of White.

Finished Size: 70 cm by 38 cm

Making Instructions:

Transfer design arranging top and bottom, right and left symmetrically on fabric.

As for the trelliswork, outline with overcast st, draw 4 threads each out from fabric at intervals of 5 fabric threads lengthwise and breadthwise, clipping threads off right at the overcast st, work trellis st referring to chart.

Work running st along the scalloped outline with 2 strands, work closed buttonhole st over, trim away the surplus.

Trelliswork

Overcast St

Overcast st

Trelliswork with 1 strand
(Draw out 4 threads at intervals of 5 threads)

Padded satin

Open cretan

Outline

Closed herringbone

Satin

Center

Satin with 6 strands

(Actual size)
With 3 strands unless specified

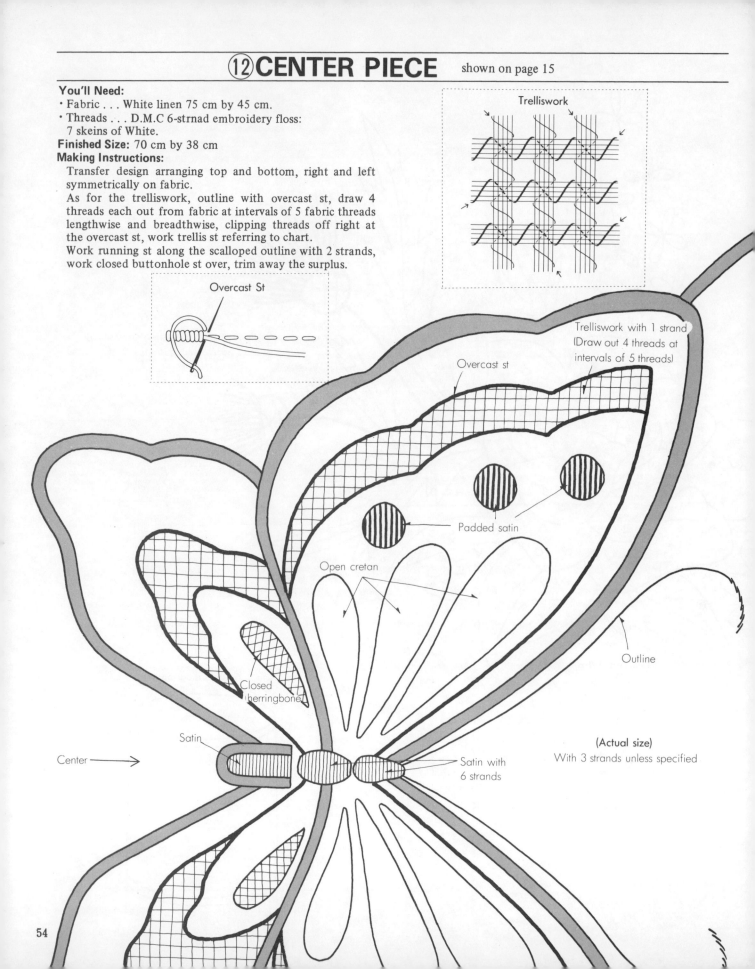

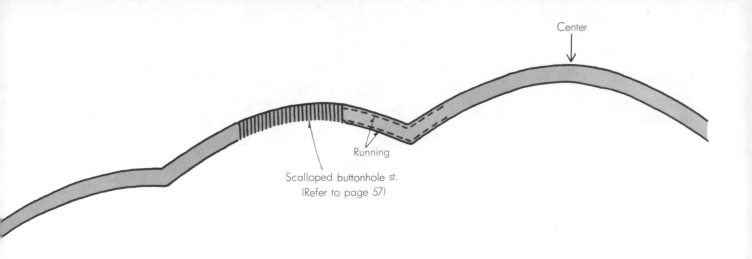

Center

Running

Scalloped buttonhole st.
(Refer to page 57)

---

④PILLOW   shown on page 5

You'll Need:
· Fabrics . . . Irish linen 30 cm square Off-White. Velveteen 90 cm by 70 cm Blue Gray.
· Threads . . . D.M.C 6-strand embroidery floss:
3 skeins of Plum (552); 2 skeins each of Raspberry Red (3689), Plum (550); 1 skein each of Episcopal Purple (915, 917, 918), Raspberry Red (3685, 3688), Plum (553, 554), Parma Violet (208, 209, 211), Ivy Green (500, 501), Pistachio Green (319) and Almond Green (502, 503); small amount of Brilliant Green (700, 702).
· Fittings . . . 1.5 cm wide Blue Gray braid 180 cm long. 36 cm long zip fastener. 44 cm square inner case stuffed with 400 g. kapok.

Finished Size: 43 cm square

Making Instructions:
Cut fabric referring to chart, copy design matching its center to that of fabric, stitch embroidery.
Sew on zip where indicated on back, place front and back right sides together, put piping strip folded in half lengthwise between, machine along so that the width of piping turns 0.5 cm.
Turn right side out, finish putting inner case into.

Piece to be Embroidered

Cutting

(Design on next page).

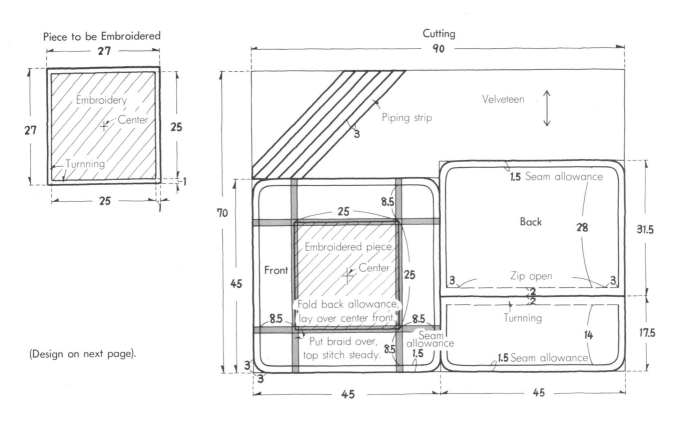

(Actual size)

= Satin st.

= padded satin st.

Long and short st unless specified.
As for long and short st, 6 strands for
outward, 5 strands for middle, 4 strands
for inward.
6 strands for satin st.

Center

Raspberry red flower

✕ = 915
⊘ = 917
⊥⊥ = 3685
÷ = 718
⊕ = 3688
⊠ = 3689
△ = 3689

Purple flower

A = 550   F = 550
B = 552   G = 552
C = 552   H = 208
D = 553   I = 209
E = 554   J = 211

Leaf

● = 500
⊙ = 319
▲ = 501
◐ = 502
○ = 503
◑ = 700
■ = 702

⑬HANDKERCHIEF shown on page 16

You'll Need:
• Fabric . . . White linen 40 cm square.
• Thread . . . D.M.C 6-strand embroidery floss:
 1 skein of White.
Finished Size: 33 cm square
Making Instructions:
 Transfer design on corner of fabric (copy encircled design on three corners), stitch embroidery.
 Running st along the scalloped edge with 2 strands, work closed buttonhole st over, cut away the surplus right at the stitch.

(Actual size)
With 1 strand unless specified.

Apply encircled design on three corners.

Eyelet with 2 strands.
(See page 67)

Satin

Long and short

Outline

Scalloped Buttonhole St

0.3 cm

Scalloped buttonhole st

Center

Running

Center

---

⑪CENTER PIECE shown on page 14

You'll Need:
• Fabric . . . White linen 91 cm by 150 cm.
• Threads . . . D.M.C 6-strnad embroidery floss:
 6 skeins of White.
Finished Size; 70 cm in diameter

Making Instructions:
 Cut out foundation piece adding 0.5 cm allowance to the size indicated on the chart, copy design matching its center to that of fabric. Cut out patch pieces with 0.3 cm allowance, shape turning allowances to wrong side with iron. Finish out-edge seaming together with patch piece, put flower pieces in place, steady with patchwork st.
 Work shadow st where indicated, stitch middle of flowers.

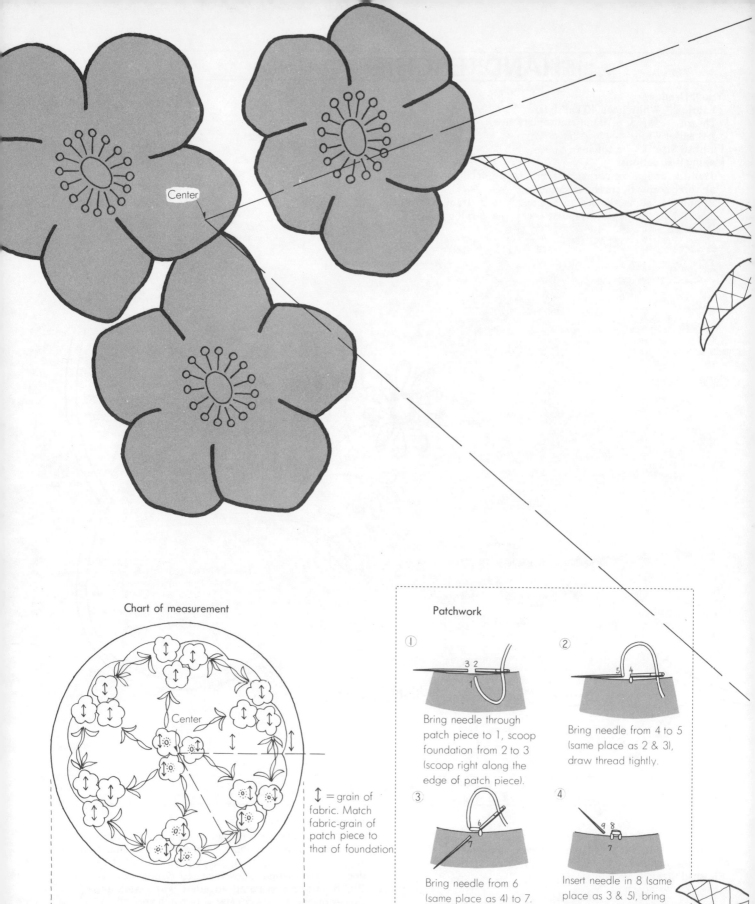

Center

Chart of measurement

Center

$\updownarrow$ = grain of fabric. Match fabric-grain of patch piece to that of foundation

70

Patchwork

① Bring needle through patch piece to 1, scoop foundation from 2 to 3 (scoop right along the edge of patch piece).

② Bring needle from 4 to 5 (same place as 2 & 3), draw thread tightly.

③ Bring needle from 6 (same place as 4) to 7.

④ Insert needle in 8 (same place as 3 & 5), bring it out to 9. Repeat 2 – 3

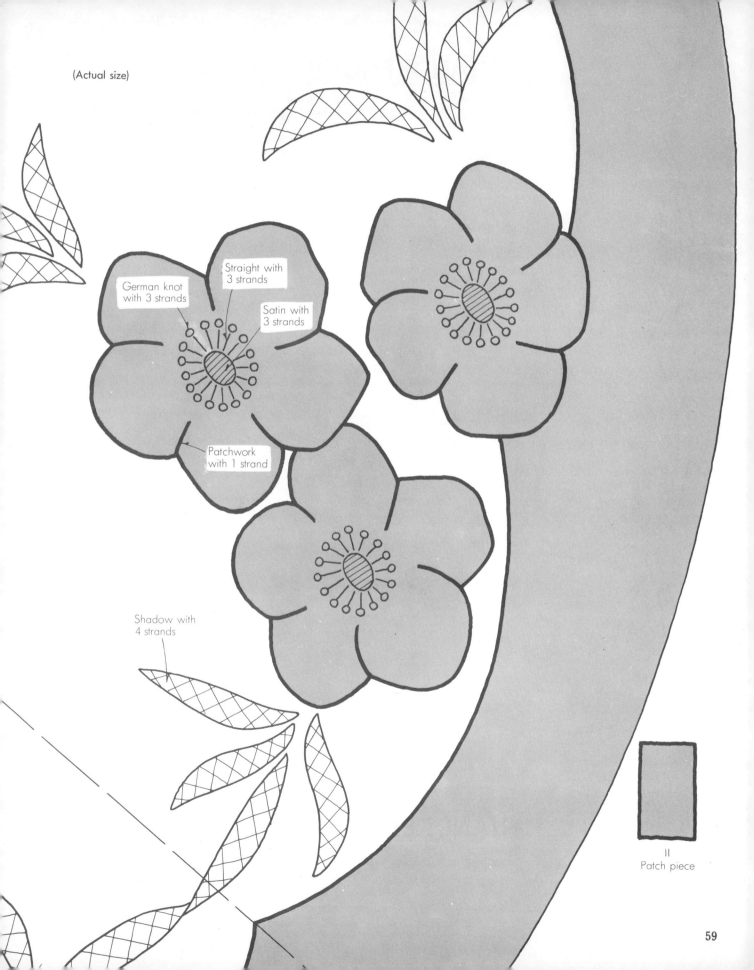

(Actual size)

German knot
with 3 strands

Straight with
3 strands

Satin with
3 strands

Patchwork
with 1 strand

Shadow with
4 strands

II
Patch piece

Center ➤

You'll Need:
· Fabric . . . White linen 40 cm square.
· Thread . . . D.M.C 6-strand embroidery floss:
  1 skein of White.
Finished Size: 33 cm square
Making Instructions:
  Transfer design on corner of fabric (copy encircled design on three corners), stitch embroidery.
  Running st along the scalloped edge with 2 strands, work closed buttonhole st over, cut away the surplus.

(Actual size)
With 1 strand unless specified.

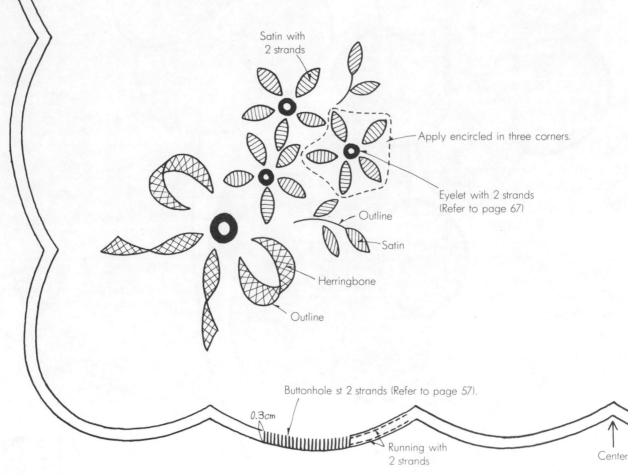

Satin with 2 strands

Apply encircled in three corners.

Eyelet with 2 strands (Refer to page 67)

Outline

Satin

Herringbone

Outline

Buttonhole st 2 strands (Refer to page 57).

0.3cm

Running with 2 strands

Center

You'll Need:
· Fabric . . . White linen 40 cm square.
· Thread . . . D.M.C 6-strand embroidery floss:
  ½ skein of White.
· Fittings . . . Crochet cotton #40, 5 g. White.
· Needle . . . Steel crochet hook size 8.

Finished Size: 34.5 cm square
Making Instructions:
  Copy design, stitch embroidery, cut the piece into 34.6 cm square in size. Fold back allowances all around, crochet along.

(Actual size)
With 1 strand unless specified.

Edging

175 sts
Work 3 sts at the corner.
Make 175 sts on each side.

0.3
1 row

French knot with 2 strands

Outline

Outline

Satin

34 cm

34.6 cm

34cm

0.3cm Turning

34.6cm

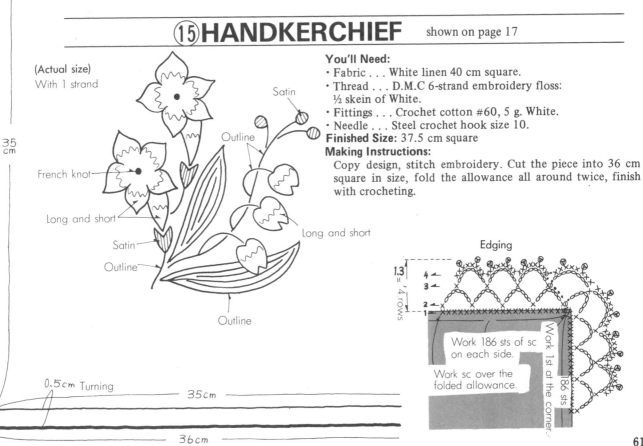

⑮ HANDKERCHIEF   shown on page 17

(Actual size)
With 1 strand

Satin

French knot

Outline

Long and short

Satin

Outline

Long and short

Outline

You'll Need:
- Fabric . . . White linen 40 cm square.
- Thread . . . D.M.C 6-strand embroidery floss: ½ skein of White.
- Fittings . . . Crochet cotton #60, 5 g. White.
- Needle . . . Steel crochet hook size 10.

Finished Size: 37.5 cm square

Making Instructions:
Copy design, stitch embroidery. Cut the piece into 36 cm square in size, fold the allowance all around twice, finish with crocheting.

35 cm

36 cm

0.5cm Turning

35cm

36cm

Edging

1.3 = 4 rows

4
3
2
1

Work 186 sts of sc on each side.

Work sc over the folded allowance.

Work 1st at the corner.

186 sts

You'll Need:
· Fabric . . . White linen 90 cm square.
· Threads . . . D.M.C Cutwork thread:
  10 skeins of white. D.M.C 6-strand embroidery floss:
  1 skein of White.
Finished Size: 83 cm square
Making Instructions:
  Transfer design on fabric referring to chart.
  Work running st along the outline 1 mm off to inward with cutwork thread 1 strand, making bars where indicated (refer to page 65), work closed buttonhole st over.

Work variation of closed buttonhole st along petals, work outline st for veins. As for the open filling in the middle of each flower, draw out fabric threads after the chain st is completed.
Fold cut edge twice, finish with one-side hem-stitching with 1 strand, mitering at each corner. Having stitched whole the design, cut away the surplus where indicated.

(Actual size)

Use stranded cotton 2 strands for chain st and trellis work, 1 strand for variation of trellis. Use cutwork thread 1 strand for the rest.

Trellis

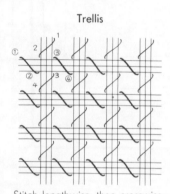

Stitch lengthwise, then crosswise.

Variation of Trellis

Variation of Closed Buttonhole St

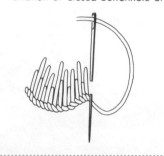

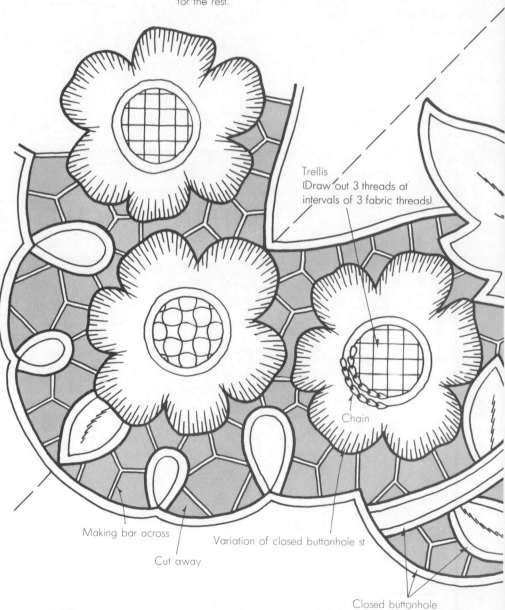

Trellis
(Draw out 3 threads at intervals of 3 fabric threads).

Chain

Making bar across

Cut away

Variation of closed buttonhole st

Closed buttonhole

Chart of measurement

Center

90

83

12

12

7   Center

One-side hemstitching
(Draw out 4 threads)

2.5

Turning   Finished line

3.5

83
90

Variation of trellis
(Draw out 3 threads at intervals of 3 fabric threads).

Closed buttonhole

Outline

Center

You'll Need:
· Fabric . . . White linen 50 cm square.
· Threads . . . D.M.C 6-strand embroidery floss:
  13 skeins of White.
Finished Size: 41 cm in diameter.
Making Instructions:
  Match center of design to that of fabric, transfer design 4 times on fabric referring to chart.
  Running st along the outline 1 mm off to inward with 3 strands, making bars where indicated, work closed buttonhole st over. Having worked whole stitch, cut away the surplus.

(Actual size)
With 3 strands

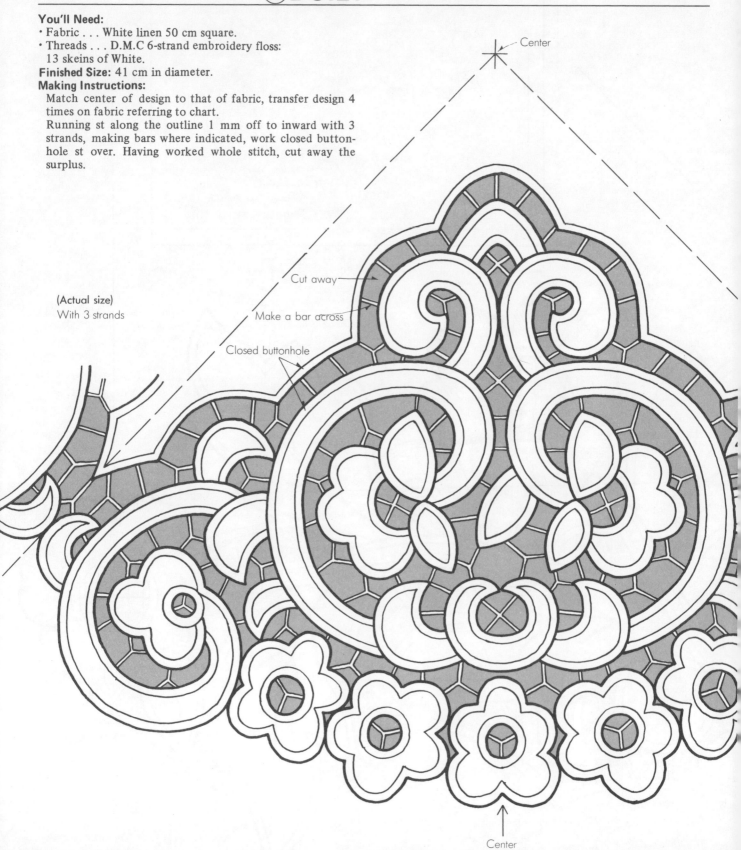

Center

Cut away

Make a bar across

Closed buttonhole

Center

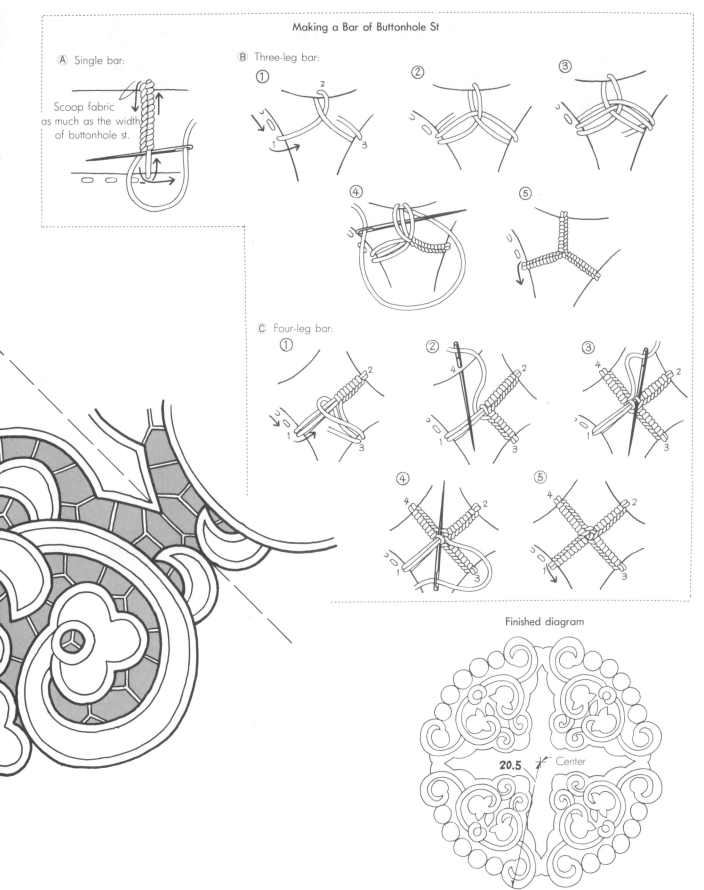

Making a Bar of Buttonhole St

Ⓐ Single bar:

Scoop fabric as much as the width of buttonhole st.

Ⓑ Three-leg bar:
① ② ③ ④ ⑤

Ⓒ Four-leg bar:
① ② ③ ④ ⑤

Finished diagram

20.5 ⟵ Center

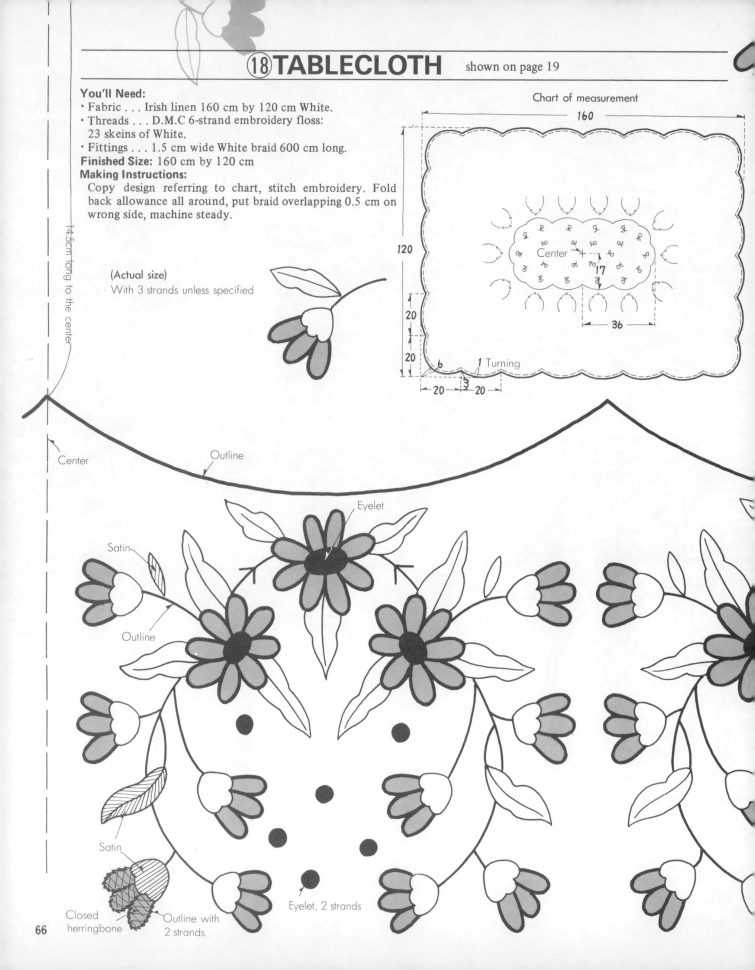

⑱TABLECLOTH shown on page 19

You'll Need:
- Fabric . . . Irish linen 160 cm by 120 cm White.
- Threads . . . D.M.C 6-strand embroidery floss:
  23 skeins of White.
- Fittings . . . 1.5 cm wide White braid 600 cm long.

Finished Size: 160 cm by 120 cm

Making Instructions:
Copy design referring to chart, stitch embroidery. Fold back allowance all around, put braid overlapping 0.5 cm on wrong side, machine steady.

(Actual size)
With 3 strands unless specified

Chart of measurement

160

120

Center

17

36

20

20

20

6

1 Turning

3

20

20

14.5cm long to the center

Center

Outline

Eyelet

Satin

Outline

Satin

Closed herringbone

Outline with 2 strands

Eyelet, 2 strands

66

Eyelets

Ⓐ Small eyelet

Ⓑ Large eyelet

You'll Need (for 2 portions):
· Fabric . . . White linen 93 cm (includes selvage) by 380 cm.
· Threads . . . D.M.C 6-strand embroidery floss:
  21 skeins of White.
· Fittings . . . 5 cm wide curtain tape 190 cm long. 16 of curtain hook.
Finished Size: 91 cm by 173 cm
Making Instructions:
  Copy two pieces of design arranging symmetrically on fabric, stitch embroidery.

Fold back the allowance on both sides, slip st steady.
Fold hem edge twice, finish with one-side hem-stitching.
Fold top edge 2 times, apply curtain tape, sew on hooks.

Back

Shadow

Satin

Closed herringbone

Shadow

Back

Shadow

Shadow
with 3 strands

Web st

Satin

Eyelet (See page 67)

㉔ FRAMED PICTURE shown on page 25

You'll Needs:

- Fabrics ... Mono canvas (10cm square of fabric = 80 meshes square) 90 cm by 60 cm Brown.
- Threads ... D.M.C 6-stand embroidery floss:
  7-1/2 skeins of Scarab Green (3.347); 7 skeins of Scarab Green (3345); 5 skeins of Scarab Green (3346); 4 skeins of Golden Green (581); 3-1/2 skeins of White; 2 skeins of Scarab Green (895); 1-1/2 skeins of Moss Green (472); 1 skein of Pistachio Green (890).
- Fittings ... Frame (45.5 cm by 36.5 cm inside). Many small and medium size round beads Brown.

Finished Size: Same size as frame.

Size of Stitch: Mesh square of design = 2-mesh square of fabric.

Making Instructions:

Copy design on the middle of fabric, work cross st with 5 stands.

Attach beads to background fabric referring to chart, set in frame.

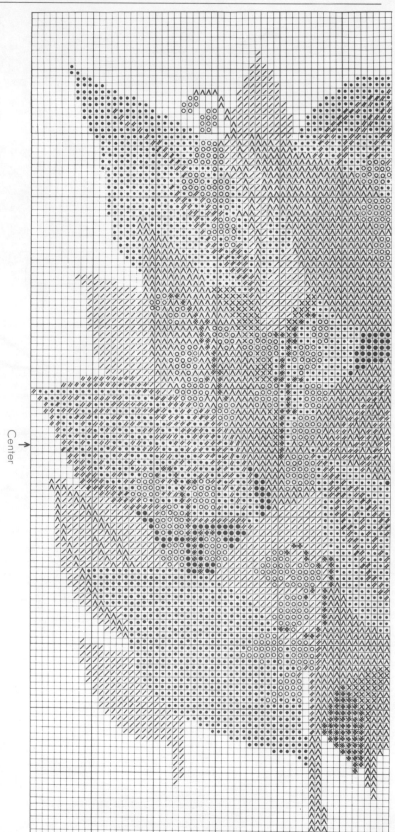

Center

To attach beads

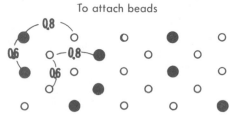

70

Center

●=890   ∧=3347   ✕=895   ∕=581   •=3345   ✳=472   ∕∕=3346   ○=White

⑳PILLOWS shown on page 21

You'll Need: (For 2 pieces)

- Fabric ... Mono canvas (10 cm square of fabric = 60 meshes by 70 meshes) 90 cm square Beige.
- Threads ... D.M.C 6-strand embroidery floss:
  6 skeins of Peacock Green (992); 3 skeins of Brilliant Green (702); 2 skeins of Beaver Gray (844); 1 skein each of Sevres Blue (798), Yellow Green (734), Umber (435), Beige Brown (839); 1/2 skein of Canary Yellow (973); Small amount of White.
- Fittings .... Knitting worsted yarn Navy Blue and Peacock Green 40 grams each. Cotton fabric for inner-bag 90 cm square White. 700 grams of kapok. Two 32 cm long zip fastner.

Finished Size: Refer to chart.

Size of Stitch: Mesh square of design = 2-mesh square of fabric.

Making Instructions:

Cut fabric in size, copy design on the middle of fabric, work cross st with 6 strands. Set zip fastner in back piece, sew out edge together with out piece, turn to right side out, put the kapok stuffed in inner-bag into.

Twist 1m long woolen yarn with 6 strands in Navy blue and Peacock green each. Sew two cords around edge, and tie the end of two cords together.

Make another pillow as same manner.

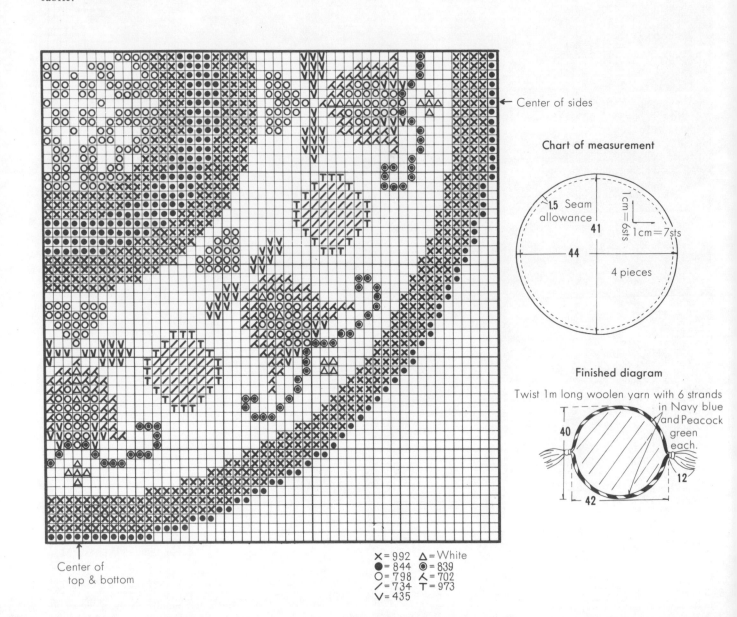

← Center of sides

Chart of measurement

1.5 Seam allowance
1cm = 6sts
1cm = 7sts
41
44
4 pieces

Finished diagram

Twist 1m long woolen yarn with 6 strands in Navy blue and Peacock green each.

40
42
12

Center of top & bottom

X = 992 △ = White
● = 844 ◉ = 839
O = 798 ʎ = 702
╱ = 734 T = 973
V = 435

72

You'll Need: (For 1 piece)

· Fabrics ... Mono canvas (10 cm square of fabric = 80 meshes square) 45 cm by 20.5 cm Light Moss Green, 72.5 cm by 45 cm Beige, 45 cm by 20 cm Dark Brown.

· Threads ... D.M.C 6-strand embroidery floss: 1 skein each of Brilliant Green (702), Moss Green (472); 1/2 skein each of Moss Green (934), Old Gold (677), Red Brown (922), Old Gold (680, 729); small amount of Moss Green (471).

· Fittings ... 0.5 cm wide Silver strip 560 cm long. 1 cm wide Golden strip 80 cm long. Inner bag stuffed with 550 grams kapok.

Finished Size: 50.5 cm by 43 cm

Size of Stitch: Mesh square of design = 2-mesh square of fabric.

Marking Instructions:

Cut fabric in size adding 1 cm seam allowance, copy design on the middle of fabric, work cross st with 4 strands.

Having worked out all stitches, sew patches together. Attach Silver strip on front with machine-stitch. Cut out one piece for back in Beige, sew front and back right sides together, turn inside out, put the inner-bag kapok stuffed into, sew opening closed.

Attach two Silver strips around edge, attach Golden strip each corner referring chart.

Chart of measurement

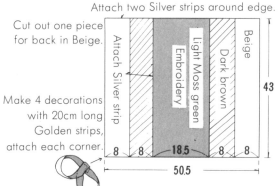

Attach two Silver strips around edge.

Cut out one piece for back in Beige.

Make 4 decorations with 20cm long Golden strips, attach each corner.

● = 934
V = 729
I = 472
◉ = 922
T = 680
O = 677
△ = 471
✕ = 702
— = White

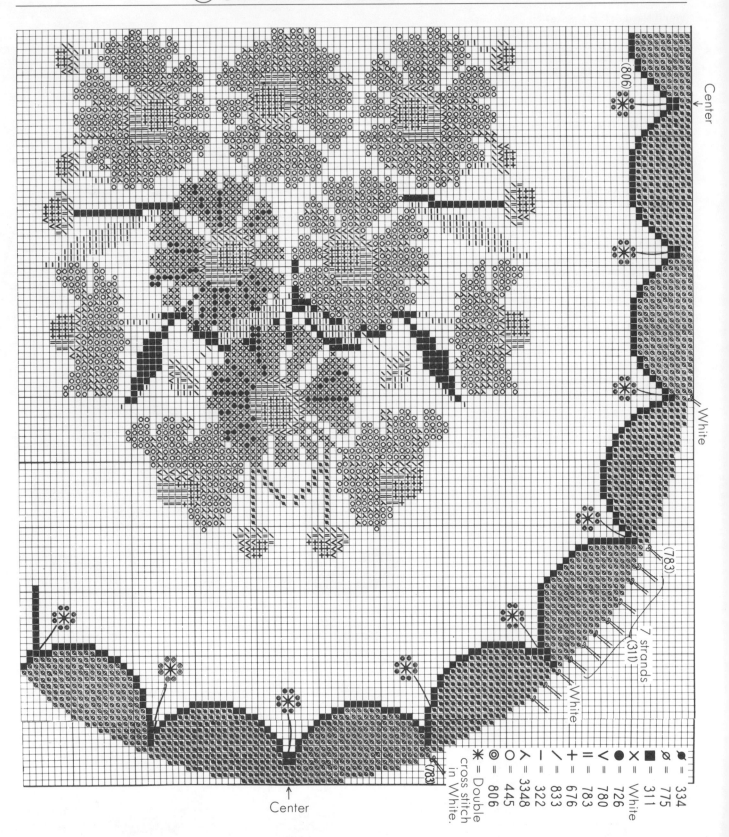

You'll Need:
- Fabric ... Mono canvas (10 cm square of fabric = 80 meshes square) 57 cm by 37 cm Light Blue.
- Threads ... D.M.C 6-strand embroidery floss:
10 skeins each of Lemon Yellow (445), Scarab Green (3348); 8 skeins of White; 7 skeins each of Azure Blue (775), Indigo (311, 334); 3 skeins each of Golden Yellow (780, 783), Copper Green (833), Old Gold (676), Indigo (322); 2 skeins each of Saffron (726) and Peacock Blue (806).
- Fitting ... Bias binding tape Blue 140 cm long.

Finished Size: 53 cm by 33 cm. Fringe 2 cm long.

Size of Stitch: Mesh square of design = 2-mesh square of fabric.

Making Instructions:
Copy design on the middle of fabric, work cross st with 5 strands symmetrically. Having worked out all stitches, finish round edge with bias binding tape.
Fold in half 5 cm long embroidery threads with 20 strands, and tie it 0.5 cm inside from edge.

Chart of measurement

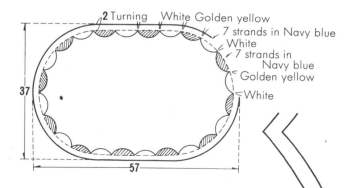

㉕ CENTER PIECE & TABLECLOTH shown on pages 26 — 27

You'll Need:
- Fabric ... Irish linen White 100 cm by 45 cm for center piece, 182 cm by 135 cm for tablecloth.
- Threads D.M.C 6-strand embroidery floss:
4 skeins of Moss Green (469); 3½ skeins of Flame Red (606); 3 skeins of Moss Green (470); 2 skeins each of Laurel Green (988), Fire Red (900), Geranium Red (892), Geranium Pink (891, 893), Peony Rose (956), White; 1½ skeins of Forget-me-not Blue (809); 1 skein each of Brilliant Green (703, 704), Coffee Brown (938); ½ skein each of Moss Green (471), Sevres Blue (798), Plum (550); small amount each of Emerald Green (954), Yellow Green (733), Saffron (725) and Poppy (666).

Finished Size: Center piece 87.5 cm by 38 cm
Tablecloth 182 cm by 128 cm

Making Instructions:
Center Piece: Transfer design on the middle of fabric referring to chart, stitch embroidery.
Running st along the scalloped edge with 2 strands, work closed buttonhole st over, cut away the surplus.
Tablecloth: Running st along the scalloped edge with 2 strands, work closed buttonhole st over, cut away the surplus right at the stitch.

Chart of measurement

Center piece

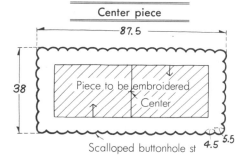

Scalloped buttonhole st

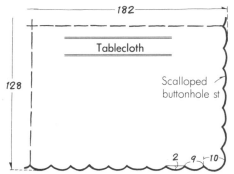

Edge of tablecloth   (Actual size)

Scalloped buttonhole st with 2 strands.
Refer to page 57.

0.4 cm

Running st with 3 strands

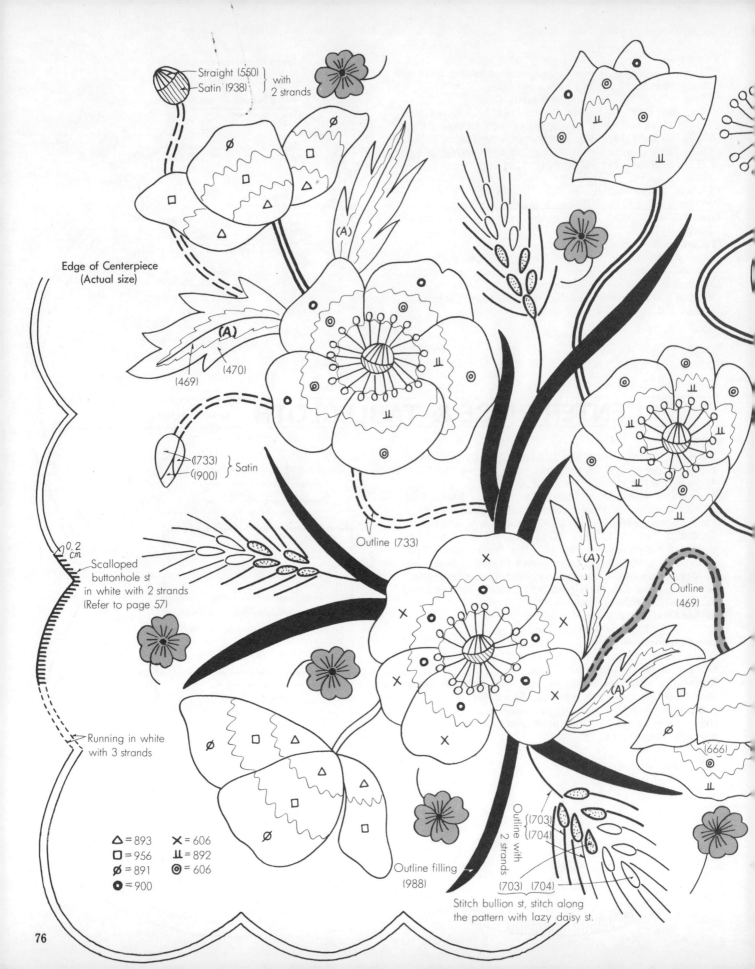

Straight (550)
Satin (938) } with 2 strands

Edge of Centerpiece
(Actual size)

(A)

(A)
(470)
(469)

(733)
(900) } Satin

Outline (733)

0.2 cm

Scalloped buttonhole st in white with 2 strands (Refer to page 57)

(A)

(A)

Outline (469)

(666)

Running in white with 3 strands

△ = 893   ✕ = 606
▢ = 956   ⊥⊥ = 892
∅ = 891   ◎ = 606
◉ = 900

Outline filling (988)

Outline with 2 strands
(703) (704)
(703) (704)

Stitch bullion st, stitch along the pattern with lazy daisy st.

76

(Actual size)
Long and short st unless specified.
With 3 strands unless specified.

(471) (470)

Outline
(470)

(A)

Center

Satin with
2 strands (938)

Straight with
2 strands
(550)

French knot
(2 times wind)
(938)

Outline
(470)

Outline with 2 strands
(938)

With 2 strands.
Satin (809)
Straight (798)
French knot (725)
(1 time wind)

Outline with
(954) 2 strands

You'll Need:

- Fabric . . . Irish linen 162 cm square White.
- Threads . . . D.M.C 6-strand embroidery floss:
  3 skeins each of Parrakeet Green (904), Scarab Green (3347); 2 skeins of Cerise (600); 1½ skeins each of Pistachio Green (320), Peacock Green (991), Garnet Red (335), Magenta Rose (962); 1 skein each of Saffron (725), Umber (435), Garnet Red (326); ½ skein each of Emerald Green (913), Saffron (726), Golden Yellow (783), Parma Violet (208, 209), Magenta Rose (963), Soft Pink (3326); small amount each of Moss Green (472) and Saffron (727).
- Fittings . . . 1.5 cm wide rickrack 520 cm long.

Finished Size: 162 cm in diameter

Making Instructions:

Referring to chart, transfer 3 patterns each of design.

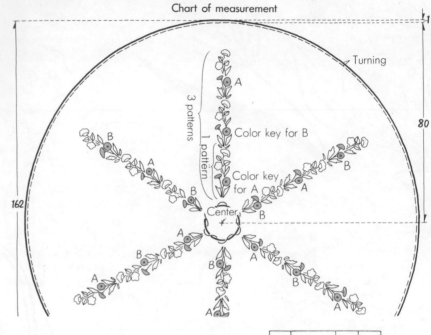

Chart of measurement

Colors	A	B
●	527	209
■	726	209
◀	725	208
△	783	725

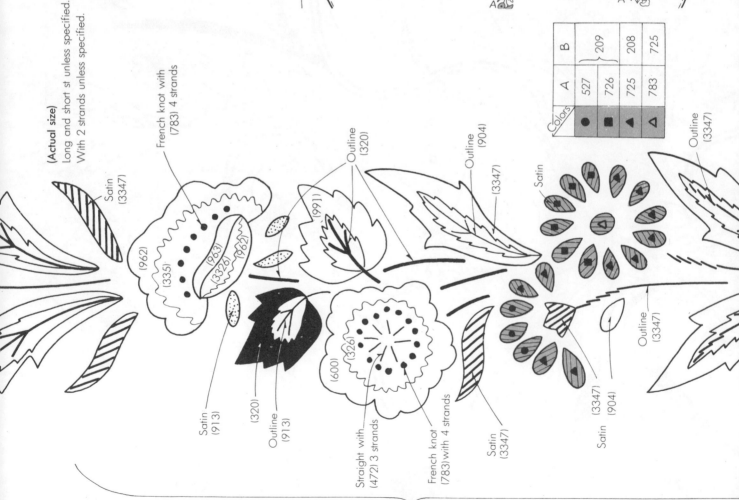

(Actual size)
Long and short st unless specified.
With 2 strands unless specified.

1 pattern

Outline filling
(435)

Outline
(3347)

14 cm diameter circle.

(904)

㉖CENTER PIECE

shown on page 28

You'll Need:
· Fabric . . . Irish linen 100 cm by 45 cm White.
· Threads . . . D.M.C 6-strand embroidery floss:
3 skeins of Pistachio Green (320); 2 skeins each of White, Pistachio Green (368), Peony Rose (956, 957), Garnet Red (309, 335), Soft Pink (899), Raspberry Red (3689); 1 skein each of Cerise (602, 603, 604), Geranium Pink (893, 894), Old Rose (3350, 3354), Soft Pink (3326, 776, 818), Indian Red (3042), Violet Mauve (327), Sky Blue (517, 518, 519), Raspberry Red (3688), Saffron (727), Light Yellow (3078), Tangerine Yellow (742, 743), Pistachio Green (369), Almond Green (502, 503, 504), Scarab Green (3347, 3348), Moss Green (471, 472), Emerald Green (913), Yellow Green (730); small amount each of Umber (436, 738), Dull Mauve (315), Terra-cotta (356), Beaver Grey (645, 647), Mahogany (402), Umber Gold (977), Golden Yellow (783) and Saffron (725).

Finished Size: 87.5 cm by 38 cm
Making Instructions:
Transfer design on the middle of fabric referring to chart, stitch embroidery.
Running st along the scalloped edge with 2 strands, work closed buttonhole st over, cut away the surplus.

Chart of measurement

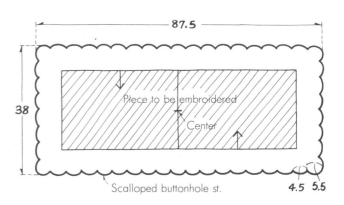

87.5

38

Piece to be embroidered

Center

Scalloped buttonhole st.

4.5 5.5

(309)

(368)

(335)

(320)

(899)

(Actual size)
Long and short st
unless specified.
With 3 strands unless specified.

A = 977
B = 402
C = 3350
D = 335
E = 309
F = 3354
G = 3326
H = 957
I = 894
J = 893
K = 956
▲ = 602
◉ = 603
V = 604
O = 3689
X = 3689
△ = 3688

I

J

H

I

J

J

K

J

Satin
(356)

J

K

J

K

K

K

J

J

J

I

I

(368)

(320)

(369)

(368)
(320)

(320)

(335)

(309)

(899)

(335)

(776)

(502)

(503)

(504)

(320)
(368)

(320)

(899)

(899)

(335)

Satin (309)

Edge (Actual size)

Running st
with 2 strands
(White)

Scalloped bottonhole st
with 2 strands
(White)
(Refer to page 57)

0.2
cm

G

◉

▲

Satin
(320)

(368)

Satin
(519)

(738)
(315) } Satin

◉

Outline (368)

Satin (519)

V

◉

V

▲

◉

(783)

(725)

Satin
(436)

(320)

(368)

Satin   Outline

(730)

V   ▲

◉   V

(327)

(3042)

French knot
(727)

(517) With 2 strands

(518)

81

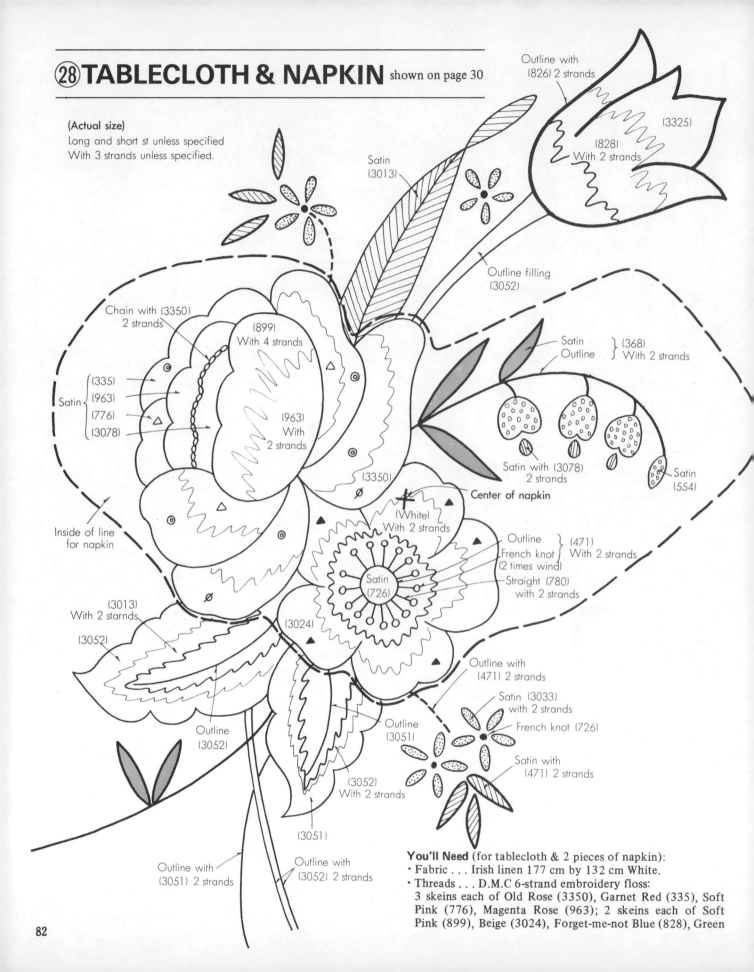

Outline with
(826) 2 strands

(3325)

(828)
With 2 strands

(Actual size)
Long and short st unless specified
With 3 strands unless specified.

Satin
(3013)

Outline filling
(3052)

Satin
Outline } (368)
With 2 strands

Chain with (3350)
2 strands

(899)
With 4 strands

(963)
With
2 strands

Satin { (335)
(963)
(776)
(3078)

Satin with (3078)
2 strands

Satin
(554)

(3350)

Center of napkin

(White)
With 2 strands

Outline
French knot
(2 times wind) } (471)
With 2 strands

Straight (780)
with 2 strands

Inside of line
for napkin

Satin
(726)

(3013)
With 2 starnds

(3052)

(3024)

Outline with
(471) 2 strands

Satin (3033)
with 2 strands

French knot (726)

Outline
(3052)

Outline
(3051)

Satin with
(471) 2 strands

(3052)
With 2 strands

(3051)

Outline with
(3051) 2 strands

Outline with
(3052) 2 strands

You'll Need (for tablecloth & 2 pieces of napkin):
· Fabric . . . Irish linen 177 cm by 132 cm White.
· Threads . . . D.M.C 6-strand embroidery floss:
3 skeins each of Old Rose (3350), Garnet Red (335), Soft
Pink (776), Magenta Rose (963); 2 skeins each of Soft
Pink (899), Beige (3024), Forget-me-not Blue (828), Green

(3051, 3052); 1 skein each of Light Yellow (3078), Moss Green (471), Golden Yellow (780), Saffron (726), Forget-me-not Blue (826), Azure Blue (3325), Plum (554), Sage Green (3013), Pistachio Green (368), Dark Brown (3033) and White.
· Fittings . . . Crochet cotton #40, 50 g. White.
· Needle . . . Steel crochet hook size 8.

Finished Size: Tablecloth 130 cm square
　　　　　　　　Napkin 46 cm square

Making Instructions:
Tablecloth: Referring to chart, copy design 8 times on fabric, stitch embroidery. Work both-side hem-stitching folding allowances all around, work crocheting over the fold.
Napkin: Copy a part of the design for tablecloth on the middle of fabric referring to chart, stitch embroidery on fabric in 6 directions, stitch embroidery. Turn cut edge all around twice to wrong side, put rickrack along overlapping 0.5 cm on wrong side, machine steady.
Finish the cut edge all around in same manner as for tablecloth.

Chart of measurement

Tablecloth

Divide 40.5 cm radius circle into eight equal parts, apply design on.

8.2

40.5

Center

132

128

Both-side hem-stitching (draw out 3 threads) before folding cut edge.

0.4

Turning

Work crocheting over the fold.

128

2

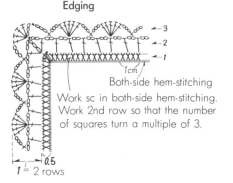

45

Napkin

45

Turning

Center

0.5 cm

44

Both-side hem-stitching (draw out 3 threads) before folding cut edge.

Work crocheting over the fold.

44

0.5

Edging

3
2
1

1cm

Both-side hem-stitching

Work sc in both-side hem-stitching. Work 2nd row so that the number of squares turn a multiple of 3.

0.5

1 = 2 rows

㉒ PILLOWS　shown on page 23

You'll Need: (For 2 pieces)
· Fabric . . . Mono canvas (10 cm square of fabric = 80 meshes square) 90 cm square Beige.
· Threads . . . D.M.C 6-strand embroidery floss:
[For A] 1 skein each of Fire Red (946), Canary Yellow (971), Episcopal Purple (718), Golden Yellow (780), Tangerine Yellow (745); Old Gold (680), Buttercup Yellow (444), Geranium Red (349); Small amount of White.
[For B] 1 skein each of Episcopal Purple (718), Peacock Blue (807), Emerald Green (912), Cornflower Blue (791), Parma Violet (209), Greenish Gray (598), Copper Green (833), Brilliant Green (704); Small amount of White.
· Fittings . . . 1.5 cm wide lace Golden brwon and Peackock Green 450 cm long each. Cotton fabric for inner-bag 90 cm square White. 700 grams of kapok.
Finished Size: 47 cm in diameter.
Size of Stitch: Mesh square of design = 2-mesh square of fabric.
Making Instructions:
[For A] Cut fabric round shape 45 cm in diameter, copy design on the middle of fabric, work cross st with 4 strands radial. Having worked out all stitches, sew front and back

right sides together, turn inside out, put the inner-bag kapok stuffed into, sew opening closed.
Sew 225 cm long Golden brown laces together double width, attach to pillow's edge with gathering stitch for border strip. Overlap 0.7 cm lace to front, and double machine-stitches.
[For B] Embroidered with indicated color, make as same manner for A. Attach with Peacock green laces for border strip.

Chart of measurement

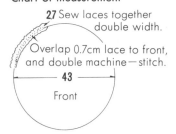

27 Sew laces together double width.

Overlap 0.7cm lace to front, and double machine—stitch.

43

Front

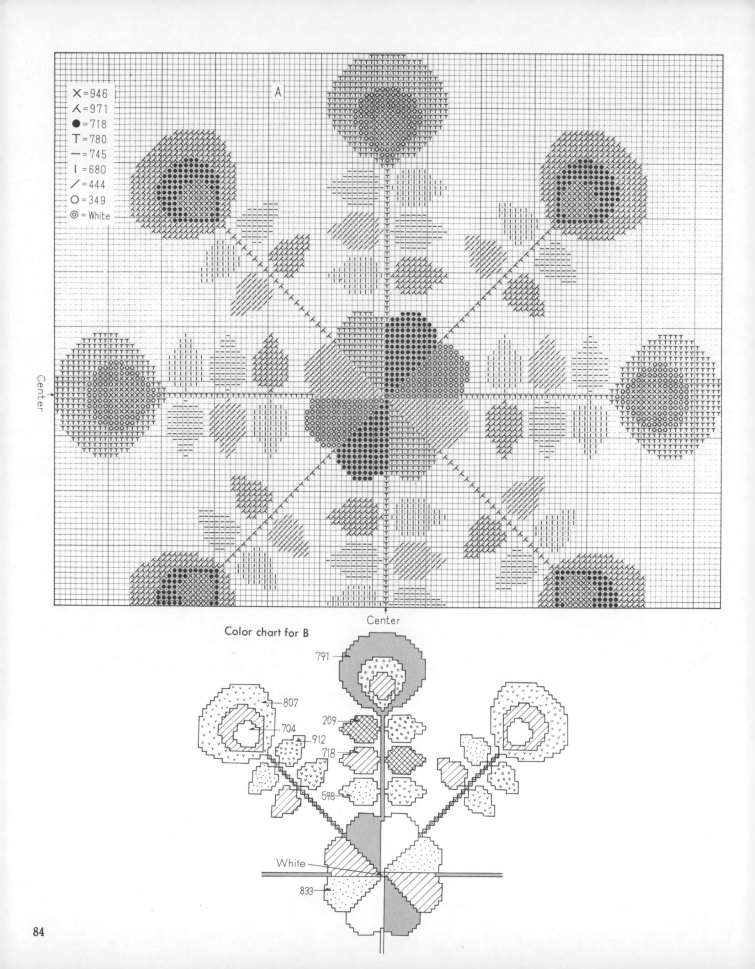

X = 946
人 = 971
● = 718
T = 780
— = 745
I = 680
╱ = 444
O = 349
◎ = White

A

Center

Center

Color chart for B

791

807
704
912
209
718
598

White
833

You'll Need:

- Fabric . . . Irish linen 172 cm by 52 cm Off-White.
- Threads . . . D.M.C 6-strand embroidery floss:

  2 skeins of Beige Brown (842); 1 skein each of Pistachio Green (367, 320, 368), Garnet Red (326, 335); ½ skein each of Forget-me-not Blue (825, 826, 827), Azure Blue (3325), Saffron (727), Soft Pink (776); small amount each of Emerald Green (912, 954, 955) and Smoke Grey (642).
- Fittings . . . 45 cm square inner case stuffed with 450 g. kapok. 2 pair of snaps.

Finished Size: Refer to chart.

Making Instructions:

Cut fabric pieces out, transfer design symmetrically on fabric, matching its center to that of front piece, stitch embroidery.

Turn the allowance of opening on back, machine 0.5 cm off the fold, sew on snaps.

Fold strips of frill in half lengthways, gather into required length, put between front and back, making ends curve, seam along, turn right side out, finish in shape.

(Actual size)
Long and short st unless specified.
2 strands for the inward of long and short st, 3 strands for the rest.

Center

Satin (727)

Outline (320)

Lazy daisy (842) Satin

Satin (955)

Satin (842)

(367)

(954) Satin (912)

(776)

(326)

French knot (727)

French knot filling (642)

(335)

Outline (367)

Outline (320)

Finished diagram

53
5 Fold 43
Frill
5
5
43 5

Cutting

172

5
5 2
13 Seam 1 allowance
Seam 1 allowance
13 Seam 1 allowance

Front
Back
Back
Frill 13
Frill 13
Frill 13
Frill 13

45 43 Seam allowance 1
Seam allowance 1
For lapping
Sew on snap
Turning lapping
For lapping
For lapping

52

Seam allowance 1

43   24   24   75
45   26   26

× = 827	⊙ = 368
△ = 3325	⊥⊥ = 320
▢ = 826	T = 367
○ = 825	

85

㉛ CENTER PIECE shown on page 34

You'll Need:
- Fabric . . . Irish linen 55 cm square Off-White.
- Threads . . . D.M.C 6-strand embroidery floss:
  2 skeins each of Umber (739), Garnet Red (309), Soft Pink (899); 1 skein each of Garnet Red (326, 335), Soft Pink (956, 818), Peony Rose (957), Sevres Blue (799), Forget-me-not Blue (809, 828), Laurel Green (988), Scarab Green (3347), Emerald Green (909, 913), Peacock Green (991), Tangerine Yellow (743) and Saffron (727).
- Fittings . . . Crochet cotton #40, 10 g. Pink, 5 g. Light Pink.
- Needle . . . Steel crochet hook size 8

Finished Size: 55 cm square

Making Instructions:

Referring to chart, transfer design matching its center to that of fabric, stitch embroidery.

Draw 1 thread out from fabric where to be folded, make 1 row of crochet along, rolling allowance in each st, crochet rows over.

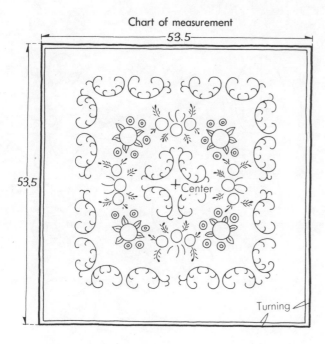

Chart of measurement

53.5

53.5

Turning

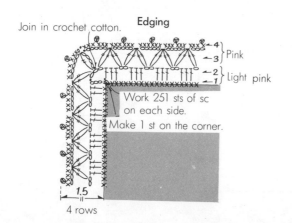

Join in crochet cotton.

Edging

Pink

Light pink

Work 251 sts of sc on each side.

Make 1 st on the corner.

1.5

4 rows

Satin

Center →

(Actual size)
Long and short st unless specified.
With 2 strands.

Ø = 899   ▲ = 309   O = 809   △ = 828
++ = 335   ◎ = 818   X = 799

Center
↓

Outline (3347)
Satin { (3347) (988)

(3347)

Satin (988)

(3347)

(909)

Outline (913)

(913)

Outline (743)
Satin

(B)

(956)
(957) (B)

(899) (956)
(A)

(309)

(326)

Satin

(991)

(991)

(913)

(991)

(913)

Satin (727)

Satin

Outline (991)

(B)

Satin } (739)
Outline

(A)

Center

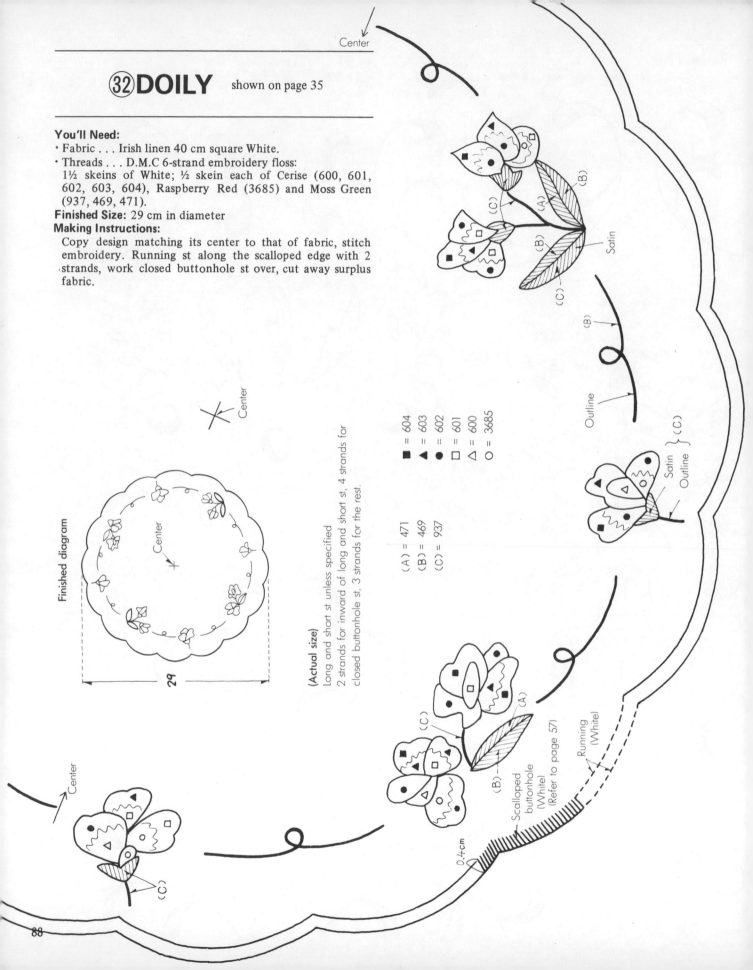

㉜DOILY   shown on page 35

You'll Need:

· Fabric . . . Irish linen 40 cm square White.

· Threads . . . D.M.C 6-strand embroidery floss:
1½ skeins of White; ½ skein each of Cerise (600, 601, 602, 603, 604), Raspberry Red (3685) and Moss Green (937, 469, 471).

Finished Size: 29 cm in diameter

Making Instructions:

Copy design matching its center to that of fabric, stitch embroidery. Running st along the scalloped edge with 2 strands, work closed buttonhole st over, cut away surplus fabric.

Center

Finished diagram

29

(Actual size)
long and short st unless specified
2 strands for inward of long and short st, 4 strands for closed buttonhole st, 3 strands for the rest.

■ = 604
◀ = 603
● = 602
□ = 601
△ = 600
○ = 3685

(A) = 471
(B) = 469
(C) = 937

Satin

(B)

(C)   (A)

(B)

(C)

Outline

(B)

Satin
Outline   (C)

Center

(C)

(C)

(B)

(A)

Scalloped
buttonhole
(White)
(Refer to page 57)

Running
(White)

0.4cm

㉚ TABLECLOTH shown on pages 32 — 33

You'll Need:

- Fabric . . . Irish linen 172 cm by 126 cm Ivory.
- Threads . . . D.M.C 6-strand embroidery floss:
  6 skeins of Moss Green (936); 5 skeins of Yellow Green (730); 4 skeins of Sage Green (3013); 3 skeins of Geranium Red (351); 2 skeins each of Morocco Red (760), Geranium Red (350); 1½ skeins each of Indigo (334), Pistachio Green (367), Umber (433); 1 skein each of Geranium Red (817), Indigo (322), Pistachio Green (320), Saffron (725); ½ skein each of Indigo (312), Azure Blue (3325, 775), Geranium Red (948) and Saffron (727); small amount of Indigo (311).

Finished Size: 160 cm by 114 cm

Making Instructions:

Transfer design on fabric where indicated, stitch embroidery. Fold cut edge twice, finish with one-side hemstitching, making corners in mitered finish.

B

(Actual size)
2 strands for inward of long and short st, 3 strands for the rest. Unless specified, stitch in same manner as for A.

(936) (730)

Long and short st

Outline
(936)

Outline (730)

Satin
(936)

(3013)
(730) } Long and short st

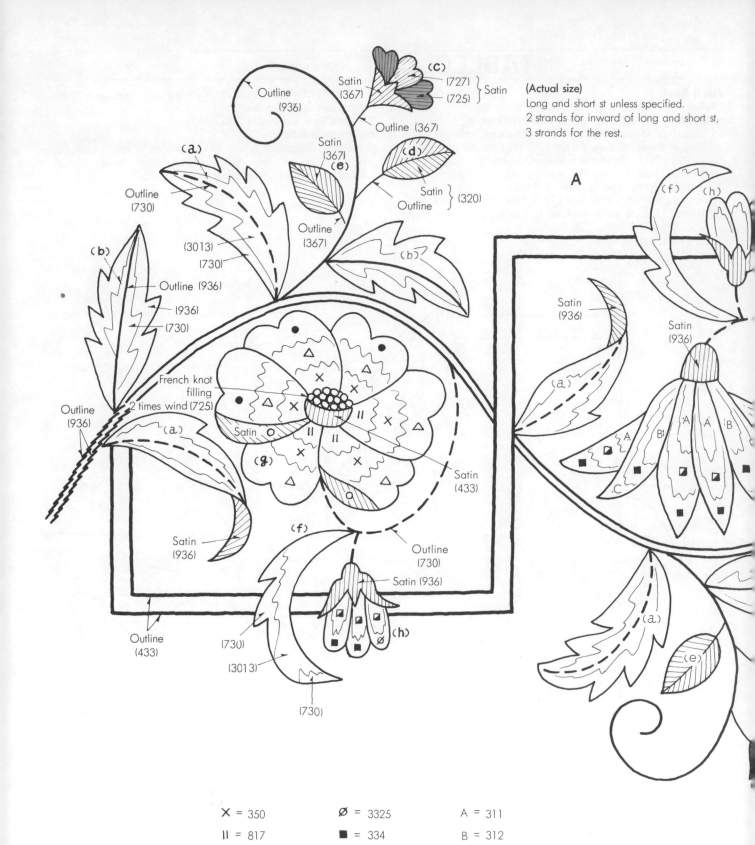

Outline
(936)

Satin
(367)

(c)

Satin
(367)

(727) } Satin
(725)

(Actual size)
Long and short st unless specified.
2 strands for inward of long and short st,
3 strands for the rest.

Outline (367)

(a)

Outline
(730)

Satin
(367)
(e)

(d)

Satin }
Outline } (320)

A

Outline (936)

(3013)
(730)

Outline
(367)

(b)

(f)   (h)

(b)

(936)

(730)

Satin
(936)

Satin
(936)

(a)

French knot
filling
2 times wind (725)

Satin   O

Outline
(936)

(a)

(g)

a

Satin
(433)

A   A   B
A   B

Satin
(936)

(f)

Outline
(730)

Satin (936)

C

(730)

(3013)

(h)

(a)

(e)

Outline
(433)

(730)

X = 350   Ø = 3325   A = 311

II = 817   ■ = 334   B = 312

● = 760   ◪ = 322   C = 775

△ = 351

O = 948

(c)

(d)

(e)

(a)

(b)

(b)

B

C

C

Satin
(936)

(a)

(e)

(d)

(c)

(b)

(d)

(h)

(f)

(c)

Chart of measurement

172

126

30

31

A'   A

B   B

A   Center   A'

3

A' and A are symmetry.

One-side
hem-stitching (Draw out 5 threads)   3

Turning   Finished line

160   6

114

6

91

You'll Need:
- Fabric . . . Irish linen 40 cm square White.
- Threads . . . D.M.C 6-strand embroidery floss:
 1½ skeins of Parma Violet (208); ½ skein each of Episcopal Purple (718), Raspberry Red (3688), Plum (550, 552, 553), Parma Violet (209, 211), Moss Green (469, 470), Light Yellow (3078) and Tangerine Yellow (743).

Finished Size: 34 cm in diameter
Making Instructions:
Transfer design on fabric, matching its center to that of fabric, stitch embroidery. Running st along the scalloped edge with 2 strands, work closed buttonhole st over, cut away the surplus.

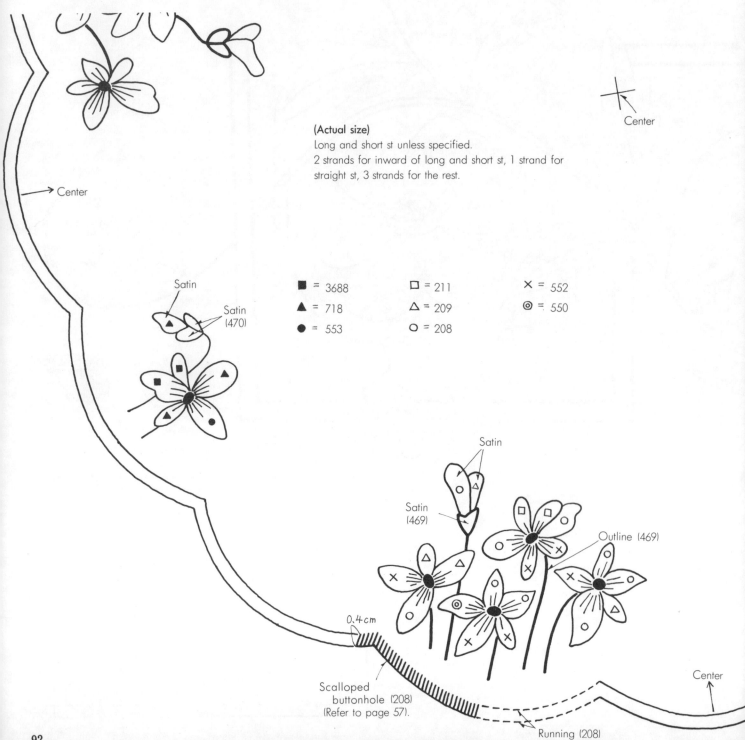

(Actual size)
Long and short st unless specified.
2 strands for inward of long and short st, 1 strand for straight st, 3 strands for the rest.

■ = 3688   □ = 211   ✕ = 552
▲ = 718   △ = 209   ◎ = 550
● = 553   ○ = 208

Satin
Satin (470)
Center
Center

Satin
Satin (469)
Outline (469)

0.4 cm
Scalloped buttonhole (208) (Refer to page 57).
Running (208)
Center

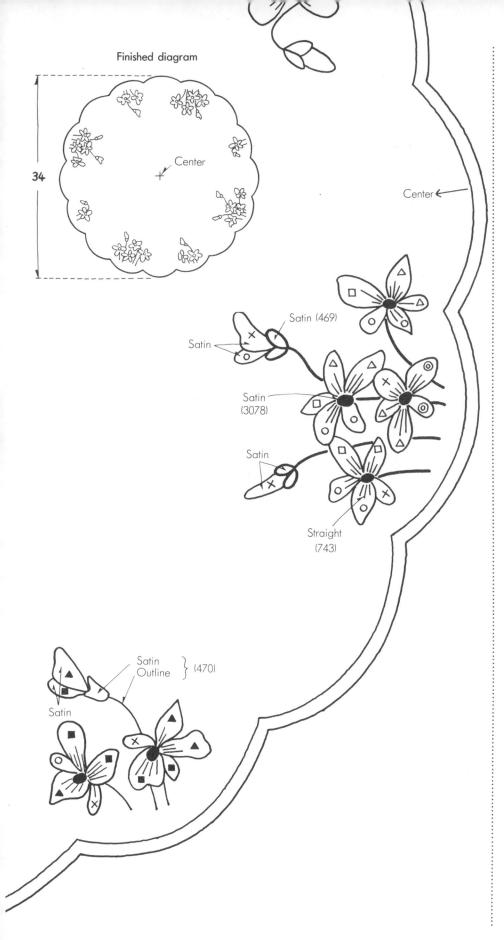

Finished diagram

34

Center

Center ←

Satin (469)

Satin

Satin
(3078)

Satin

Straight
(743)

Satin
Outline } (470)

Satin

㉞ PILLOW CASE & PIECESPREAD

shown on page 36

You'll Need:

· Fabric . . . Irish linen White 182 cm by 67 cm for pillow case, 158 cm by 79 cm for Piecespread.

· Threads . . . D.M.C 6-strand embroidery floss:

Pillow Case

2 skeins of Soft Pink (818, 819); 1½ skeins of Soft Pink (776); 1 skein each of Peony Rose (956, 957), Geranium Pink (893, 894), Emerald Green (913), Moss Green (966), Saffron (727), Light Yellow (3078), Parma Violet (209, 211), White, Smoke Grey (644); small amount each of Emerald Green (912, 954, 955), Pistachio Green (320), Sevres Blue (800), Forget-me-not Blue (828), Beige (3047) and Soft Pink (899).

Piecespread

2 skeins of Soft Pink (776, 818, 819); 1 skein each of Peony Rose (956, 957), Geranium Pink (893, 894), Soft Pink (899), Emerald Green (912, 913, 954, 955), Moss Green (966), Pistachio Green (320), Saffron (727), Light Yellow (3078), Parma Violet (209, 211); small amount each of Sevres Blue (800), Forget-me-not Blue (828), White, Beige (3047) and Smoke Grey (644).

Finished Size:

Pillow case 74 cm by 54 cm
Piecespread 144 cm by 68 cm

Making Instructions:

Pillow case: Referring to chart, cut fabric in size, transfer design on front piece, stitch embroidery. Draw out fabric threads 0.3 cm in width where indicated on front piece, work hem-stitching over, making each corner in mitered finish. Place A over B, turn allowance to wrong side, secure to wrong side of front, making hem-stitching along.

93

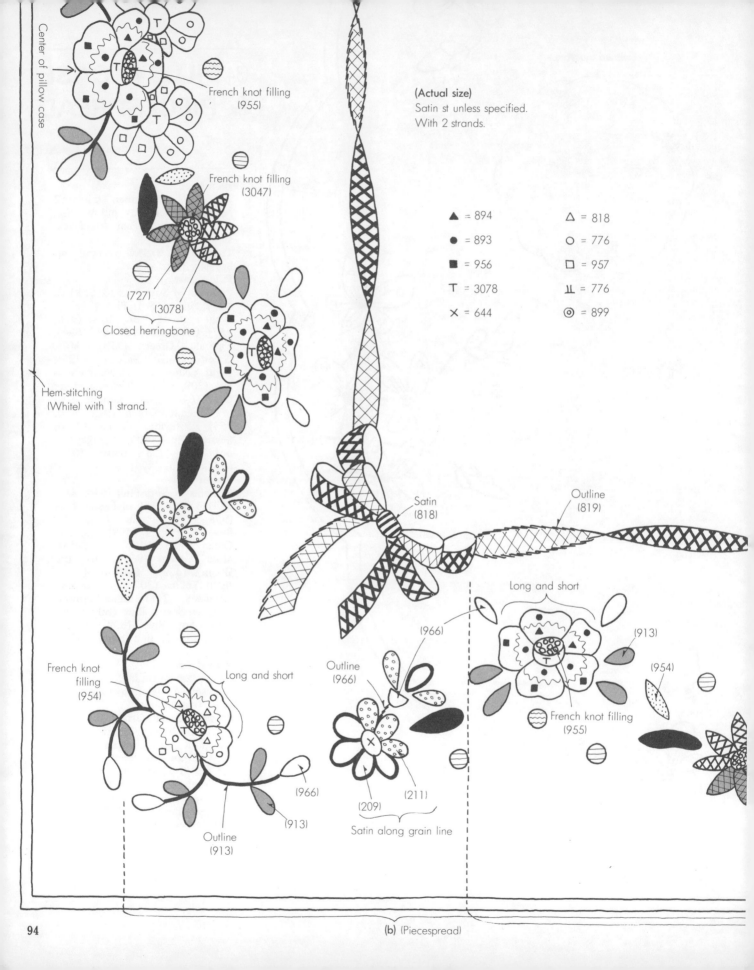

Center of pillow case

French knot filling
(955)

French knot filling
(3047)

(727)
(3078)
Closed herringbone

Hem-stitching
(White) with 1 strand.

French knot
filling
(954)

Long and short

Outline
(913)

(966)

(913)

(Actual size)
Satin st unless specified.
With 2 strands.

▲ = 894   △ = 818

● = 893   O = 776

■ = 956   ▢ = 957

T = 3078   ⊥ = 776

✕ = 644   ◉ = 899

Satin
(818)

Outline
(819)

Long and short

(966)

Outline
(966)

(211)

(209)

Satin along grain line

(913)

(954)

French knot filling
(955)

94

(b) (Piecespread)

(819) (818)

Closed herringbone

(828)

French knot filling

(3047) (644)

Long and short

French knot filling
(955)

(800)

Outline
(966)

(912)

(966)

(320)

(a) Repeat (a) 3 times for piecespread.

Center of pillow case

95

Cutting & Measurement

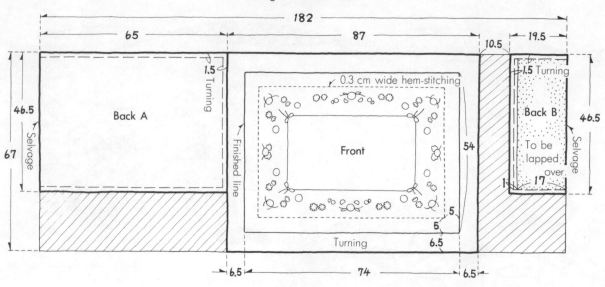

Piecespread: Copy design on fabric referring to chart, stitch embroidery. Fold the allowance top edge into 2 cm wide, slip st steady. Work 0.3 cm wide both-side hem-stitching on three sides, making corners in mitered finish.

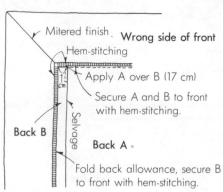

Mitered finish. **Wrong side of front**

Hem-stitching

Apply A over B (17 cm)

Secure A and B to front with hem-stitching.

Back B

Selvage

Back A

Fold back allowance, secure B to front with hem-stitching.

Work hem-stitching with 1 strand White.

Piecespread

Chart of Measurement

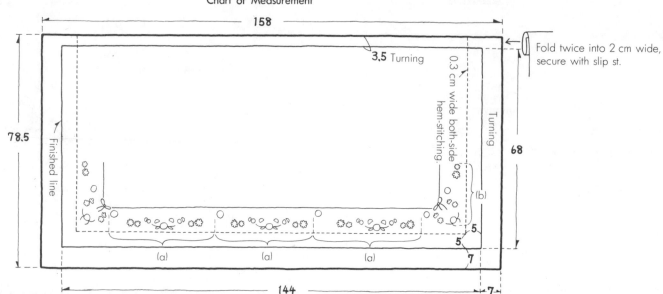

Fold twice into 2 cm wide, secure with slip st.

㉟ PILLOW shown on page 37

You'll Need:
- Fabrics . . . Irish linen 93 cm by 45 cm Pink. Broad cloth 90 cm by 40 cm Dark Pink.
- Threads . . . D.M.C 6-strand embroidery floss:
1 skein each of White, Índigo (334), Azure Blue (3325, 775), Peony Rose (956), Soft Pink (776), Plum (552, 554), Cerise (601, 604), Episcopal Purple (718), Raspberry Red (3688), Tangerine Yellow (740, 743), Aprikot Pink (945), Buttercup Yellow (444), Saffron (727), Light Yellow (3078), Emerald Green (913), Ivy Green (501), Almond Green (502, 503), Laurel Green (988), Scarab Green (3347), Moss Green (4701); small amount each of Flame Red (608), Tangerine Yellow (741), Violet Mauve (327), Garnet Red (309, 335), Raspberry Red (3689) and Moss Green (966).
- Fittings . . . 38 cm long zip fastener. 44 cm square inner case stuffed with 450 g. kapok. Small amount of heavy weight yarn.

Finished Size: Refer to chart.

Making Instructions:
Cut fabric pieces out, copy design on front, stitch embroidery.
Sew zip on back, seam into pillow. As for the decoration, join 4 strips together, seam into pipe, draw gatherings, secure in place.

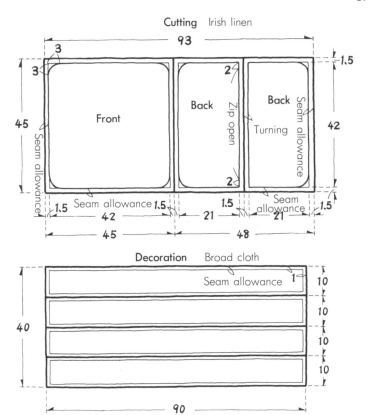

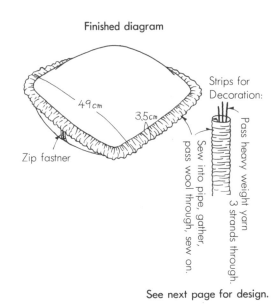

See next page for design.

(Actual size)
Long and short st unless specified.
With 3 strands.

Outline (988)

(775)

(3325)

(334)

(A)

(A)

Outline filling
(988)

Outline
(470)

Straight
(988)

Satin
(470)

Satin
(3347)

French knot
(327)

Satin
(3347)

(A)

Satin
(327)

Satin
(470)

(470)
(988)

(A)

(B)

Outline filling
(913)

Satin
(3347)

(988)

(B)

Center

(B)

Outline
(502)

Outline
(966)

Outline
(503)

Satin (913)

Outline
(913)

Satin
(503)

Chain (608)
Fly (740)
Satin (3347)
Satin (White)
Satin { (945) (743)
Satin (740)
Satin (604)
Satin Ø
Satin (501)
Satin (502)
Satin (502)
Straight (502)
Satin (503)
Outline (913)
Satin (502)
French knot (608)
(741)
Satin { Outline } (503)
(470) (501)
Outline

✕ = 776
▢ = 956
△ = 604
○ = 601
⊙ = 3689
Ø = 3688
◐ = 718
▲ = 554
■ = 552
◫ = 309
∨ = 335

✳ = 727
Ⴎ = 444
⊤ = 3078

㊱ VIOLET

You'll Need:
- Fabric . . . Irish linen 20 cm square Ivory.
- Threads . . . D.M.C 6-strand embroidery floss:
  small amount each of Cornflower Blue (792, 793), Forget-me-not Blue (827), Plum (552), Parma Violet (208, 209, 211), Moss Green (470), Laurel Green (986, 988), and Tangerine Yellow (743).
- Fittings . . . Frame (12 cm square inside). 12.7 cm square cardboard.

Finished Size: Same size as frame.
Making Instructions:
Copy design on the middle of fabric, stitch embroidery. Lay embroidered piece over the cardboard, turning the surplus to wrong side, fix in frame.

(Actual size)
Long and short st unless specified.
2 strands for inward of long and short st, 3 strands for the rest.

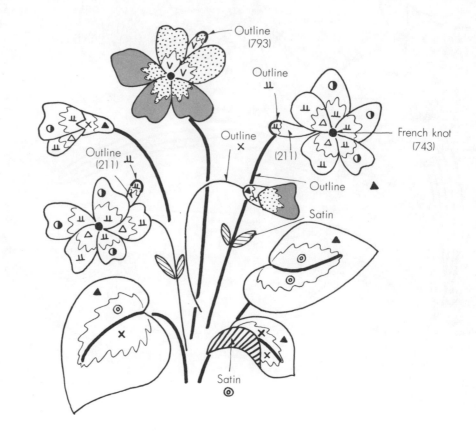

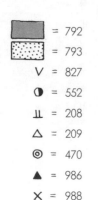

= 792
= 793
V = 827
◑ = 552
Ⅱ = 208
△ = 209
◎ = 470
▲ = 986
✕ = 988

㊲ CARNATION

You'll Need:
- Fabric . . . Irish linen 20 cm square Ivory.
- Threads . . . D.M.C 6-strand embroidery floss:
  small amount each of Scarlet (815, 304), Turkey Red (321), Geranium Red (351), Garnet Red (335), Soft Pink (776, 819), Ivy Green (501) and Almond Green (502, 504).
- Fittings . . . Frame (12 cm square inside). 12.7 cm square cardboard.

Finished Size: Same size as frame.
Making Instructions:
Copy design on the middle of fabric, stitch embroidery. Lay embroidered piece over the cardboard, turning the surplus to wrong side, fix in frame.

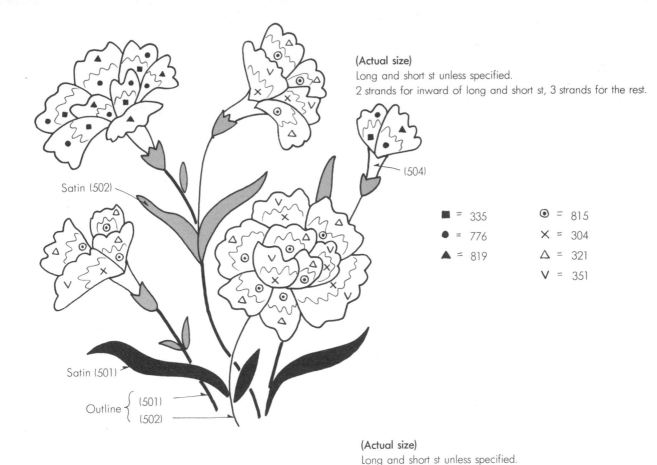

(Actual size)
Long and short st unless specified.
2 strands for inward of long and short st, 3 strands for the rest.

Satin (502)

(504)

■	=	335	⊙ =	815
●	=	776	✕ =	304
▲	=	819	△ =	321
			V =	351

Satin (501)

Outline { (501)
          (502)

(Actual size)
Long and short st unless specified.
2 strands for inward of long and short st, 3 strands for the rest.

△	=	718
⊙	=	3688
V	=	3689
O	=	3689

㊳ PRIMROSE

You'll Need:
· Fabric . . . Irish linen 20 cm square Ivory.
· Threads . . . D.M.C 6-strand embroidery floss:
½ skein of Respberry Red (3689); small amount each of Ivy Green (500, 501), Almond Green (502), Episcopal Purple (718), Raspberry Red (3688), Laurel Green (986, 988), Parrakeet Green (904) and Saffron (726).
· Fittings . . . Frame (12 cm square inside). 12.7 cm square cardboard.
Finished Size: Same size as frame.
Making Instructions:
Copy design on the middle of fabric, stitch embroidery. Lay embroidered piece over the cardboard, turning the surplus to wrong side, fix in frame.

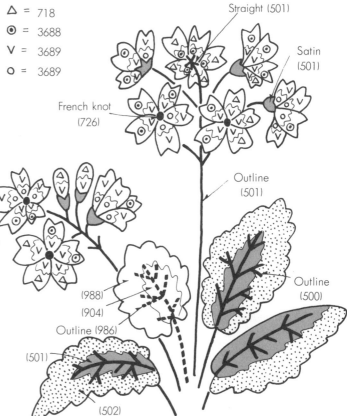

Straight (501)

Satin (501)

French knot (726)

Outline (501)

Outline (500)

(988)
(904)
Outline (986)
(501)
(502)

101

㊴ COSMOS

You'll Need:
- Fabric . . . Irish linen 20 cm square Ivory.
- Threads . . . D.M.C 6-strand embroidery floss:
  small amount each of White, Cerise (600, 602, 603, 604), Scarlet (814), Laurel Green (986, 988), Parrakeet Green (904) and Tangerine Yellow (743).
- Fittings . . . Frame (12 cm square inside). 12.7 cm square cardboard.

Finished Size: Same size as frame.
Making Instructions:
  Copy design on the middle of fabric, stitch embroidery. Lay embroidered piece over the cardboard, turning the surplus to wrong side, fix in frame.

(Actual size)
Long and short st unless specified.
2 strands for inward of long and short st, 3 strands for the rest.

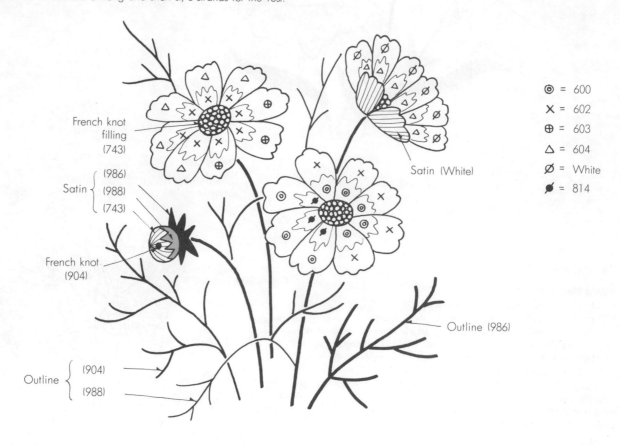

French knot filling (743)

Satin { (986) (988) (743)

French knot (904)

Satin (White)

Outline (986)

Outline { (904) (988)

◉ = 600
✗ = 602
⊕ = 603
△ = 604
∅ = White
✿ = 814

㊵ SWEETPEA

You'll Need:
- Fabric . . . Irish linen 20 cm square Ivory.
- Threads . . . D.M.C 6-strand embroidery floss:
  ½ skein of Pistachio Green (320); small amount each of Plum (552), Parma Violet (208, 209, 211), Canary Yellow (972), Tangerine Yellow (743), Light Yellow (3078) and Pistachio Green (367).
- Fittings . . . Frame (12 cm square inside). 12.7 cm square cardboard.

Finished Size: Same size as frame.
Making Instructions:
  Copy design on the middle of fabric, stitch embroidery. Lay embroidered piece over the cardboard, turning the surplus to wrong side, fix in frame.

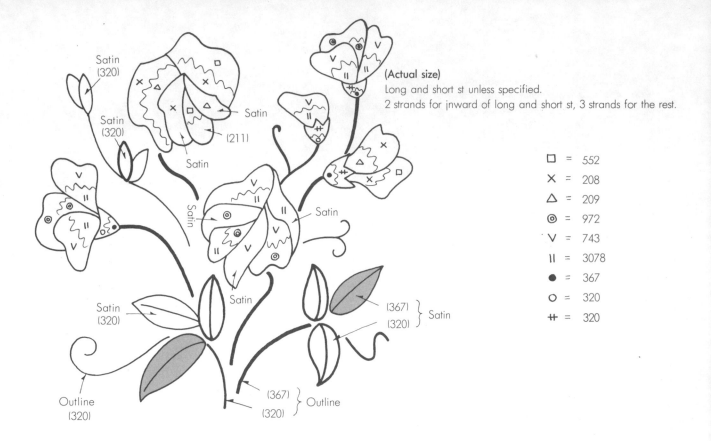

Satin
(320)

Satin
(320)

Satin

Satin
(211)

Satin

Satin

Satin

(Actual size)
Long and short st unless specified.
2 strands for inward of long and short st, 3 strands for the rest.

□ = 552
✕ = 208
△ = 209
◎ = 972
V = 743
ll = 3078
● = 367
O = 320
⧺ = 320

Satin
(320)

Satin

(367)
(320) } Satin

Outline
(320)

(367)
(320) } Outline

(Actual size)
Long and short st unless specified.
With 3 strands unless specified.

④¹ THISTLE

You'll Need:
· Fabric . . . Irish linen 20 cm square
Ivory.
· Threads . . . D.M.C 6-strand embroidery
floss:
small amount each of Episcopal Purple
(718), Raspberry Red (3688, 3689),
Plum (552, 553, 554), Green (3051,
3052) and Pistachio Green (319, 367,
320, 368)
· Fittings . . . Frame (12 cm square inside).
12.7 cm square cardboard.
Finished Size: Same size as frame.
Making Instructions:
Copy design on the middle of fabric,
stitch embroidery.
Lay embroidered piece over the cardboard, turning the surplus to wrong
side, fix in frame.

Ø = 367
O = 320
✕ = 368
◎ = 3052

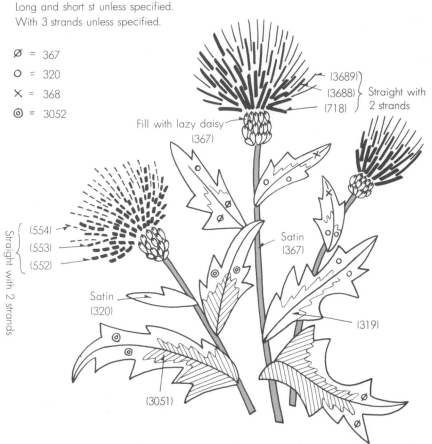

(3689)
(3688) } Straight with
(718) } 2 strands

Fill with lazy daisy
(367)

Straight with 2 strands
(554)
(553)
(552)

Satin
(367)

Satin
(320)

(319)

(3051)